Snowboarding

Snowboarding

EFFIN OLDER

STACKPOLE
BOOKS

Published by
STACKPOLE BOOKS
5067 Ritter Road
Mechanicsburg, PA 17055
www.stackpolebooks.com

Printed in China

10 9 8 7 6 5 4 3 2 1

FIRST EDITION

Cover design by Wendy Reynolds
All photos by the author

Library of Congress Cataloging-in-Publication Data
Older, Effin.
      Snowboarding/Effin Older.—1st ed.
          p.   cm.
      ISBN 0-8117-2931-1
      1. Snowboarding. I. Title. II. Title: Snowboarding.
GV857.S57 O53 1999
796.9—dc21

                                                        99-17541
                                                            CIP

To Jules, my lifelong riding partner

Contents

CHAPTER FOUR: WHEN BODY MEETS BOARD

CHAPTER FIVE: GETTING GOING

CHAPTER SIX: BEYOND THE BLUE

CHAPTER SEVEN: TRICKS AND TREATS

CHAPTER EIGHT: CHRIS AND JIM'S EXCELLENT TUNING

CHAPTER NINE: STAYING IN TOUCH

SNOWBOARD TRIVIA

Acknowledgments

Thanks to everyone who helped me with this book.

Special thanks to Julie Vickery, for teaching me the joy of riding; Steve Ash, Irwin Benkert, Greg Bock, Jim Broda, Sal Contreras, Paul Graves, David Lines, Jim McDowell, Amber Older, Jules Older, and Kevin Senft, for riding with me, giving me great advice, and critiquing the manuscript; Sabrina Sadeghi, for demonstrating how to stay fit for safe, fun riding; Jim Wood and Chris Mask, for sharing their knowledge of snowboard maintenance; Smugglers' Notch Ski Resort, for letting Julie take time off from directing their snowboard school to teach me to ride; Burton Snowboards, Dr. Bone Saver, Fila, Leedom, Louis Garneau USA, Rossignol, Skeletools, Spin Factor, and Spirakut, for supplying snowboard gear for testing and photographing; and finally, Barbara Thomke and Bob Mulcahy, for keeping the competitive spirit alive!

Introduction

THE POWER OF ENVY

Envy made me do it. Pure envy.

As an alpine skier, for years I'd watched snowboarders carve long, graceful, arcing turns, swooping across the snow like eagles gliding on air. As they carved, they seemed to float, gravity-free, on the pencil-thin edge of their board. It looked magical. I wanted to float, to defy gravity, to swoop like an eagle.

But could I?

There was only one way to find out.

I hung up my skis and got onboard.

I wasn't alone. In the ten years between 1987 and 1997, the number of snowboarders had nearly quadrupled—from a million to almost four million. What began in the 1960s as a sport for young, male nonconformist types now included women, children, and elders.

As excited as I was about learning to ride, one thing scared me—the prospect of getting hurt. Stories of body slams and face plants were rife. Since I've never been into pain, neither maneuver sounded the least bit enticing. Plus, I'd already seen firsthand the body of a battered boarder. It was not a pretty sight.

Several years ago my husband took up snowboarding. Six times he went, and six times he came back, body bruised and ego battered. Finally, on the advice/command of his physical therapist—and his wife—he stopped. Remembering his pain, I had to wonder, Was I crazy? Did I really want to enroll in the *sport de torture?*

I did. Not only that, I somehow persuaded my husband to give it another try.

LOOKING FOR MR. GOODBOARD

I knew my first job was to find a suitable teacher. I also knew from my years of taking ski lessons that not all instructors are created equal. Mine had to have three qualities:

First was the ability to speak plain, clear English. I was all too familiar with ski instructions like "Driving your outside downhill arm to the outside will pull your upper body out over your downhill ski." Sure.

Second, my instructor had to have patience. "Just get out there and rip, dude," wasn't my style. Yes, I needed to be challenged, but, no, I didn't want to be flung way outside my comfort zone.

And third, my instructor had to have a sense of humor. I was about to learn a new sport in a very public place. There would be times when I would look uncool and uncoordinated, probably even stupid. But it didn't matter, as long as I could laugh at myself and my instructor could laugh with me, not at me.

My search led me to Julie Vickery, a Level 2 AASI (American Association of Snowboard Instructors) certified instructor and supervisor of the snowboard program at Smugglers' Notch Resort in northern Vermont. She's a top-notch rider and a top-notch teacher.

My instructor, Julie Vickery, demonstrating a perfect carve.

At the start of our first lesson, I mentioned my fear of getting hurt. Julie looked at me quizzically. "That's the old school," she said. "You're not going to fall in my class."

"I'm not?" I asked with a mixture of relief and disbelief.

I knew lots of people who had spent their first two or three lessons falling and hurting themselves in the No Pain–No Gain School of Riding. The result? Most gave up.

Julie smiled. "In the early days, when instructors were just learning the sport themselves, and equipment was in the infant stage of development, there were lots of bruised butts. Not so today."

I can't say that I never fell in Julie's class. It would be nearly impossible to learn a sport like snowboarding without falling. In the beginning, I could just be standing on my board, not moving, and suddenly find myself sitting on my butt. Even Julie later admitted, "After my first day of riding with my husband as my instructor, that night he slept on the couch!"

But it's absolutely true that face plants and body slams were not part of my experience. And they needn't be part of yours. Whether you're seven, seventeen, or fifty-seven, you can learn to ride the no-bruise way and have the time of your life.

Julie said one other thing as we walked to the beginners' slope for that first lesson: "Today is going to change the rest of your life."

She was right. The change began with my whoop of exhilaration after I felt it for the first time—that feeling of floating, as though gravity had taken a break. Granted, I didn't look like a swooping eagle, but I sure felt like one. And the feeling just keeps getting better and better.

ABOUT THIS BOOK

There is nothing mysterious about learning to snowboard. If you like being out on a mountain in winter, and if you're reasonably fit, there's no reason why you shouldn't try it. Plus, if you come from a surfing, skiing, or skateboarding background, you already have an advantage—you have a good sense of what it feels like to balance on a slippery surface. And balance is one of the key ingredients in snowboarding.

But don't mistake this advantage for thinking that you should pick up a snowboard and head for the top of the mountain on your first day. This could—no, this will—result in sore body parts.

Like any sport, snowboarding has basic techniques and skills that you should learn in the beginning. This book lays out those skills in chapters 4 and 5. After reading those chapters, you'll have a good idea of the fundamentals, from straight gliding on your board, to getting on and off lifts, to linking your first turns.

The order in which I discuss the skills is the same order in which Julie taught them to me. One skill builds on another. In your eagerness to learn how to snowboard, you may be tempted to skip some steps. Try to resist this temptation. Be patient, and practice each skill until you feel at least moderately comfortable with it—you'll progress much faster in the long run. Of course, there's no law against sneaking a look ahead at basic techniques for riding the halfpipe, but if you dash for the pipe before you've mastered the falling leaf, you could be in for some surprises. Ouch!

Besides guiding you through the basic steps of snowboarding, this book helps you select the right equipment for your kind of riding and the right clothing to keep you warm and dry. It shows you how to care for your body (including the right way to fall) and how to care for your board (including hot and cold waxing). You'll learn techniques for riding moguls (bumps), powder, and in the trees. You'll hear professional skiers like Heidi Voelker, tennis pro Martina Navratilova, and humorist Dave Barry talk about their snowboarding experiences.

And here's a bonus. Once you've read this book, you can impress your friends with your knowledge of snowboard trivia. For example: Can they name the snowboarding legend who was a stunt double for Agent 007? Do they know who introduced the idea of the high back binding? Can they name the halfpipe trick that features a 540-degree rotation? You can. Or soon will be able to.

Besides instruction from Julie, you'll read tips from other top instructors and riders around the country: riders like halfpipe pro Sabrina Sadeghi. For her advice on getting fit and staying fit, check out her exercises in chapter 3. And for tips on mastering moguls, turn to chapter 6, where instructor Greg Bock shows how it's done.

Reading this book about snowboarding is one way to learn the fundamentals of the sport. But you don't want to just read about it, you want to do it. The fastest, safest, and easiest way to go is to combine your reading with taking lessons. And I don't mean from your good buddy George, who taught himself to ride. Yes, I know George will teach you for free, and yes, I agree he's a way cool dude. But George has some bad habits that you don't want to pick up now and have to unlearn later. Take lessons, either privately or in a group, from a certified snowboard instructor.

Here's a story. Julie and I are riding up the chairlift. As always, I study every snowboarder under the liftline. When I first started lessons, I could tell a beginner from a really good rider, but I couldn't point out what made the difference other than that one looked awkward and clumsy and the other, smooth and graceful. Then, one day, Julie said, "See that guy. He's self-taught."

I looked, trying to figure out how she knew.

Then she pointed to another. And another. "See how they're jerking their upper bodies around to make their boards turn. And look at their arms flailing all over the place. They're wearing themselves out, using far more energy than they need to. They'll be exhausted by the time they get down the hill."

Julie pointed to still another snowboarder. "That one's had lessons."

Suddenly, the difference was obvious. This rider had a quiet upper body, no jerky movements, no flailing arms. Her riding looked effortless and elegant. She appeared to be using no energy at all.

The benefit of taking lessons is that when you start to develop bad habits, your instructor will correct you on the spot. You won't keep repeating poor techniques that make your learning harder than it needs to be. And here's the best part: Most people need just two or three lessons to master the basics. After that, it's a matter of putting on miles. And miles and miles. When you feel you're ready to move on to a new skill, then it's time to take another lesson.

Once you've read this book and signed up for your first lesson, remember this: Snowboarding is about having fun. And just as there's no one right way to have fun, there's no one right way to ride. Some riders look for the deepest powder, some for the biggest air, some for the fastest race time. Some, like me, just want that feeling of soaring like an eagle. It's up to you. Once you've mastered the basics, you'll soon discover your own technique and style—your own way to have fun.

Go for it!

I

Birth of the Board

The next time you strap on your snowboard with its sintered base, thermo-plastic inserts, glass reinforced cap, and state-of-the art graphics, stop and consider this.

It's the early 1960s. Winter. In Muskegon, Michigan, Sherman Poppen is nailing two old skis together for his kids to play on. Half a continent away, in East Brunswick, New Jersey, Paul Graves is shooting a hill on a single, fat Norwegian ski wearing his galoshes. Over in Haddonfield, New Jersey, Tom Sims is feeling frustrated because he can't skateboard on the snow-covered street. So, having already made skateboards and skimboards (for skimming across his swimming pool), Sims holes up in his garage and bangs together a ski-board for riding on snow. He hammers a sheet of aluminum to the bottom of a wooden board and attaches a strip of carpet with U-nails to the top. For bindings, he uses clothesline. Sims later replaces the clothesline with a more sophisticated binding—bicycle innertubing.

Meanwhile, in White Plains, New York, nineteen-year-old surfer Dimitrie Milovich gets together with his friend, Wayne, and starts making boards for riding on snow. His first board is fashioned from redwood and weighs about 45 pounds—not much fun to haul around. Milovich soon moves on to lighter, foam-core boards. He laminates gravel to the top to keep his feet from slipping. Later, he replaces the gravel with nylon straps that fit over the top of his feet.

From the 45-pound redwood, Milovich went on to develop the original Winterstick boards. Tom Sims started Sims Snowboards. Paul Graves experimented with board designs and dedicated himself to promoting snowboarding. And Sherman Poppen? Those two skis he nailed together for his kids became the prototype for the Snurfer.

Two of Sherman Poppen's Snurfers. Note the staples used for traction and the crude leather bindings.

At the mention of a Snurfer, many people of a certain age grin, recalling that they probably still have one tucked away somewhere in the attic. (If you're among them, don't be tempted to use it for firewood—it's an increasingly valuable collector's item.) Poppen's Snurfer was a narrow plywood board with a cord attached to the slightly upturned front tip. Staples along the top surface provided the only traction for boots. The rider held on to the cord for the wild trip down the hill—wild because without metal edges or sidecut, the Snurfer was nearly impossible to steer or stop. Most riders came to a graceless end by wiping out in a spectacular spill.

As crude as the Snurfer was, over a million were sold. Most people considered them nothing more than a toy. But even a toy can spur a competition, and that's just what happened. Loosely organized Snurfer competitions sprang up wherever there was a hill to climb up and ride down. One such hill was at Muskegon Community College. The rules of the competition were simple—the winner was the rider who made it to the bottom in the fastest time.

Jake Burton Carpenter showed up for the 1979 Muskegon race, but not with a Snurfer tucked under his arm. Jake Burton had his own slightly longer, slightly wider board outfitted with rubber cup bindings, the kind you see on water skis. This radical new design departure immediately threw the race organizers into a tizzy. Should this unknown renegade rider with his souped-up Snurfer be allowed to

High-tech bindings, Snurfer-style.

compete? After much gnashing of teeth, Jake Burton was allowed to enter in his own special "open" category. He was the only contestant.

He won.

No one could have guessed on that day in 1979 that Jake Burton would go on to own the most successful snowboard business in the world.

BIRTH OF FREESTYLE

Paul Graves—the guy in East Brunswick on the fat Norwegian ski— also entered the 1979 Muskegon race. He had been riding Snurfers and promoting snow surfing since the early '60s. At the 1979 race, Graves did something the Snurfing world had never seen. Instead of riding a straight line down the course, Graves added 360-degree spins on snow and in the air. He finished the race with a dramatic front-flip dismount. In those few brief moments, freestyle boarding was born.

Graves lost the race, but he was named National Freestyle Snurfing Champion for 1979. Like Jake Burton, he was alone in his class.

"It felt great to win the title," Graves remembers, "but I felt something was missing. We needed recognition that snow surfing was a legitimate sport, not just a crazy fad. I knew people like Jake Burton,

Tom Sims, and Dimitrie Milovich were dedicated to the sport, but they were all working independently of each other in their own separate parts of the country. There was no communication among them. I wanted to change that."

Graves figured the best way to do it was to hold a competition—but not just for Snurfers and not on a back hill at a community college. His competition would be open to all riders, and it would be held, for the first time, at a ski resort. Because he had now moved from New Jersey to Woodstock, Vermont, Graves had his sight set on Woodstock's Suicide Six Ski Area.

He approached the town's outdoor recreation department. "It was a fight," Graves recalls. "Suicide Six was reluctant to have it there. But even though they weren't happy, they did work with us. They made us hold the race on The Face, one of the steepest pitches at that area. I think it was to see us fail."

The year was 1982. Over one hundred competitors from the United States and Canada came to participate in the National Snow Surfing Championship, the first of its kind at a ski area. Competitors were allowed to race on anything that was strapped to their feet. Most raced on Snurfers wearing rubber boots or tennis shoes.

There were two events: the downhill and the slalom. Unlike the one-rule snow-surfing competition in Michigan, this time there were three rules for entrants: Each competitor had to buy a lift ticket. Each competitor had to have a retention device to keep the board from running away. (Most riders simply tied one end of a piece of rope around an ankle and screwed the other end to the board.) The winner was the fastest one down the hill after two runs.

Tom Sims won the downhill and walked away with the $300 first prize.

That was the beginning of the National Snow Surfing Championships at Suicide Six. It was also the end. After watching rider after rider careen out of control down The Face, Suicide Six banned the race from their mountain.

In spite of the ban, Paul Graves considered the event a success. But it was the first and last time he would run a snow-surfing championship. He and his wife, Denise, who was now five months pregnant, had worked for eleven long months putting the event together. They were burned out and broke. Graves gave the event to Jake Burton.

Paul Graves preparing to "snurf" The Face at Suicide Six Ski Area
in Woodstock, Vermont.

The following two years, Jake Burton held the competition at Snow Valley in southern Vermont. Then, in 1985, he moved it to Stratton Mountain, Vermont. That's where it stayed, and it has subsequently grown into the premier snowboarding competition in the world, the U.S. Open.

After the Suicide Six race/debacle, snowboarding had a long way to go before it would be accepted as a mainstream sport at ski areas. The image of out-of-control Snurfers was hard to forget. But snowboard manufacturers weren't sitting on their hands. Innovators like Jake Burton, Tom Sims, and Dimitrie Milovich were constantly improving their boards to make them safer and more controllable. Steve and Dave Derrah, two brothers from Rhode Island, began producing boards with metal edges. Jeff Grell introduced the concept of the high back binding, which gave support to a rider's knees and ankles for heel-side turning.

But even with the equipment improvements, many ski areas remained reluctant to open their doors to snowboarders. Who were these newcomers, anyway? They had their beginnings in skateboarding and surfing, not skiing. They not only were younger, but they appeared to be, shall we say, less respectable to the established skiing community. They wore drab, baggy outfits instead of brightly colored, form-fitting one-piece snowsuits. They boasted about "ripping arcs off high banks" and "sticking big airs"—concepts meaningless to skiers. And both feet were buckled in sideways on one short, fat board rather than straight ahead on two long, skinny ones. It was a clash of two snow cultures.

But the snub from the ski areas didn't dampen the snowboarders' enthusiasm. They continued to hold competitions and to attract more and more enthusiasts to the sport. The numbers of snowboarders grew rapidly. And in light of louder and louder demand, ski area managers were forced to take another look. Slowly, more and more began to allow boarders onto their slopes. But not always without restrictions.

Longtime snowboarder David Lines recalls what he had to go through in the 1980s at Jay Peak ski area in northern Vermont. "Before I could buy a ticket, I had to be tested by a snowboard instructor. It was an on-the-spot, on-slope assessment of my skills. I had to ride with the instructor on a green [easiest] run, then on a blue [intermediate] run, and if I passed those two, I could try a black [expert] run. I'd be given a green, blue, or black pass, depending on how I did. If anyone was caught riding on an unapproved trail, he'd get his pass pulled and promptly be invited to leave the mountain."

"I tried snowboarding partly out of curiosity, and partly because I was hosting a television show on learning how to snowboard—and I was the guinea pig. I have never been slammed so hard so many times in a sixty-minute period and still come back for more. But after that first hour, I was linking turns fairly easily.

"It's harder and harder to get a rush out of skiing—it's more automatic to me than walking. On a snowboard, I get a rush even on a beginners' slope. The thing I love about snowboarding is that it turns a slope that would be boring on skis into excitement."

—Lisa Feinberg Densmore,
television commentator for skiing and snowboarding,
U.S. ski team 1976–79, Pro Tour racer 1985–90

YOU'VE COME A LONG WAY, DUDE

Snowboarding has grown up since the days of the Snurfer. Its adolescent bad-boy image is being replaced by the sight of young children, women, and senior citizens slipping on their helmets for a day on their boards. Hard-core skiers are trying the sport for the first time, and many are finding it as much fun as skiing. Some, more fun! Snowboard manufacturers continue to improve the comfort and safety of their boards, boots, and bindings. The ease and convenience of the strapless binding hold great appeal for both young and older riders.

Although acceptance of snowboarders has come grudgingly, almost every resort now welcomes them, and as more and more people experience how easy it is to learn to ride—the learning curve really is steep—acceptance will continue to grow. Many now see snowboarding as a shot in the arm that will benefit the whole snow sport industry. The irony is not lost on those early snowboarders who were banned from ski areas.

You couldn't find a better example of how attitudes toward snowboarders have changed than to talk with Pat O'Donnell, chairman and CEO of Aspen Skiing Company. After years of skiing, at fifty-nine, O'Donnell began snowboarding. "I took up snowboarding as a new learning adventure. Once I got through the beginning stage and made that breakthrough to start feeling fluid, it was like I died and went to

"I said I'd never snowboard. I thought snowboarders were just a bunch of punks. I didn't like their image and I never wanted to be involved with them. Then I was traveling with my husband to a ski area that had a lot of flats. We were there for four days and I knew I'd be bored. I was recovering from a knee injury and just getting back into skiing. There were companies demoing snowboards, so I said, 'Hey! I might as well try it here, where it's flat.' So I took a private lesson. After about an hour on the baby hill, I was linking turns. That afternoon, I went to the top of the mountain.

"I never took bad falls, even in the beginning, because I understood from skiing about staying on my edges. Never ride on a flat board. That's when you catch an edge. Actually, the way I carve on my board is very similar to the way I carve on my skis. But I do more tricks on the board than on skis. This is my second season, and I'm now in the halfpipe.

"I wouldn't give up skiing. That's my job. I'm a ski racer six days a week at Deer Valley, and one day a week I'm Snowboard Betty. I love it."

—Heidi Voelker,
three-time Olympic skier and
1995 National Giant Slalom Champion

heaven. Any falls I had in the beginning were worth it in the long run. Boarding in powder is magical, a dream come true. I still haven't got back on my skis."

Now that snowboarding has become a medal sport in the Winter Olympics, there is every reason to believe that the growth of the last few years will continue. And that there will be many more Pat O'Donnells. If the past is a predictor of the future, we are seeing just the first spurt of a major eruption.

2

Gearing Up to Ride

The first time you walk into a snowboard shop, be prepared to be overwhelmed. You'll see a gazillion boards of different lengths and widths. You'll see soft boots and hard boots. You'll see bindings with straps and bindings without straps. The selection is huge, the choices daunting. How can you possibly walk out with the right equipment for you?

Easy. Read this chapter. It takes the mystery out of boards, boots, and bindings. By the way, I'm not suggesting that you go out and buy all new equipment for your first day on the slopes. Renting is a better way to go until you know you like snowboarding enough to make a sizable financial investment. Later in this chapter I'll talk about renting, when to stop renting, and how to save money when buying new or used equipment.

TYPES OF SNOWBOARDING

The equipment you should buy depends on the type of snowboarding you plan to do. There are three types: freestyle, freeride, and racing (also referred to as carving or alpine riding). Because they sound so similar, everybody always confuses freeride and freestyle. So I'm getting rid of freeride. From now on, it's called *all-mountain* to distinguish it from freestyle.

Freestyle. Freestyle riders spend most of their time in the halfpipe or the snowboard park. The halfpipe is that long, U-shaped trough where riders execute aerial flips, twists, and spins. The snowboard park is a specially designed area with big jumps and man-made obstacles like logs and handrails for boarders to bounce, spin, or slide off.

All-Mountain Riding. All-mountain riding means doing pretty much whatever you want to do when you want to do it. It can be cruising down groomed trails, swooping through trees, shooting over bumps, hitting on jumps, carving perfect turns, or floating weightlessly through deep powder.

Racing. Racers specialize in carving precision turns at high speeds. They compete against each other and the clock.

BODY PARTS

Freestylers, all-mountain riders, and racers each use different boards. Before we see how they differ, let's first look at how they're alike. They all have the following:

Tip. The front of the board. It's also called the nose.

Tail. The rear end of the board. Freestyle and all-mountain boards have upturned tails; racing boards have tails that are flatter and more squared-off.

Edge. A narrow strip of sharpened steel that runs all the way around the board. This steel strip is what helps you grip the snow so

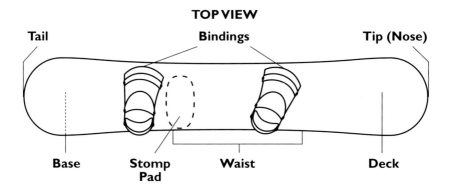

TOP VIEW

Tail — Bindings — Tip (Nose)

Base — Stomp Pad — Waist — Deck

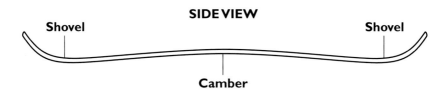

SIDE VIEW

Shovel — Shovel

Camber

that you can turn and stop. During your first lesson, the instructor will refer to your heel edge and your toe edge. When you're standing on your board, the toe edge is the edge nearest to your toes. The heel edge is the edge nearest to your ————. You got it!

Base. The bottom of the board.

Deck. The top of the board. It has predrilled holes to mount bindings.

Stomp Pad. A rubber pad that sticks to the deck in front of the back binding. It keeps your back foot from slipping around on your board when it's not strapped in, like when you're getting off a lift or sliding across a flat area. Racing boards typically don't have stomp pads.

Shovel. The curved-up area near the tip and tail.

Waist and Sidecut. If you stand your board on its tail, you'll see that it's narrowest in the middle. This curved midsection is the waist. The curve is the result of sidecut.

Flex. The ability of a board to bend lengthwise. You can test a board's flex by standing it on its tail, holding the tip firmly in one hand, and bending it in the middle with your other hand.

Camber. The raised middle section of the board when it's lying flat on the ground. Camber is what distributes a rider's weight evenly along the entire edge of the board. Without camber, the board may act squarely and may not hold well on ice due to uneven pressure spots. Without camber, the board won't track well.

TYPES OF SNOWBOARDS

Snowboards are designed to do a variety of things, from spinning through the air to carving fast turns to floating through waist-deep powder. Just as there are three basic types of snowboarding, there are three basic types of snowboards: freestyle, all-mountain, and racing.

Freestyle. These boards are turned up at the tip and tail, so they can be ridden backward as well as forward. Riding backward—that is, riding with your back foot in the lead—is called riding fakie or switch. Freestyle boards are shorter and wider than other types of boards— shorter for spinning and jumping; wider because freestylers mount their bindings straight across the board, perpendicular to the edge. With a narrower board, their toes would hang over the edge. These boards have a soft flex, making them easy to turn and good for beginners. They're ridden with soft boots.

All-Mountain. Like freestyle, all-mountain boards are upturned at both ends. They perform well in powder and hard-packed snow and can

From left: racing, freestyle, and all-mountain boards

be ridden in the halfpipe and snowboard parks. All-mountain boards are slightly longer, narrower, and stiffer than freestyle boards, but they are still good for beginners. Riders usually mount their bindings on an angle rather than straight across the board. Typically, they choose soft boots.

Racing. These boards are easy to distinguish from their freestyle or all-mountain cousins by their flatter tip and squared-off, almost totally flat tail. Racing boards are longer, stiffer, and narrower at the waist than freestyle and all-mountain boards. Their narrow waist makes it easier to go from edge to edge when carving high-speed turns. Their longer length means more edge contact with the snow. More edge on the snow means it takes more energy to turn the board, but it also means that the board holds more securely at high speeds. Hard boots are usually worn with carving boards.

BOOTS AND BINDINGS

Selecting the right board is just one of the decisions you'll make when putting together your equipment package. You also need a boot and binding system. As with boards, it's best to try out different combinations, but no matter what boot you end up with, my advice for beginners is to *start in soft boots.* Even if you're a skier and are used to hard boots, start soft. Why? Because soft boots are so darn comfortable. You can walk around in them, go shopping, even drive your van.

There are now boots designed for women's narrower feet, heels and lower calf muscles. Unfortunately, most rental shops stock few pairs of women's boots, so if you're renting, you may get stuck with men's boots.

There are three basic boot and binding setups: soft boots and strap bindings, soft boots and step-in bindings, and hard boots and plate bindings. Simply put, bindings attach you to the board. Strap bindings are the most popular.

Soft Boots. Soft boots are made from a combination of waterproof leather and canvas uppers and a thick rubber tread that gives good traction for walking. They have padded liners that can be removed for drying. Soft boots close with laces; some have straps for additional tightening. These boots allow the ankle and foot movement for freestyle and soft snow riding.

Hard Boots. Hard boots have a tough plastic outer shell that's hard to the touch. Like soft boots, they have removable padded inner liners. Unlike soft boots, they close with adjustable buckles, not laces. These are not boots for beginners. Because of their stiffness, the ankles have less movement and the boot/board interface is more rigid and precise. This means your mistakes will be more noticeable. Hard boots are used mainly by racers and carvers.

Strap Bindings. These are also called freestyle bindings and are used with soft boots. They have a high back and two straps; one fits over the top of the ankle, the other over the toe. For extra control, some styles have a third strap around the shin.

Soft boot

Hard boot

Step-in Bindings. A relatively new soft-boot alternative to the strap binding, the step-in eliminates the hassle of buckling and unbuckling straps. It's a particularly attractive system for beginners whose balance is still a bit shaky and for older riders who can't easily bend down. Some designs are just a flat plate and a locking device; others also incorporate the high back of the strap binding.

Plate Bindings. These are designed for hard boots. The boot is held firmly in place at the toe and heel. These bindings are favored by racers and high-speed carvers.

Soft boot and strap binding

Step-in boot and binding

Hard boot and plate binding

DRESSING FOR THE MOUNTAIN

Dressing for the mountain means being prepared for weather changes, snow condition changes, and your own body temperature changes. The way to do it is to dress in layers so that you can easily peel off a garment on warm spring days and add layers on frigid midwinter days. The three-tier system has become the standard model for layering.

Inner Layer. This is the wicking layer, next to your skin. Wear a long-sleeved top and long underwear made of polypropylene or a similar material that dries quickly and draws moisture away from your body. *Do not wear cotton.* Cotton holds moisture and dries slowly—just the opposite of what you want.

Middle Layer. This is the layer that keeps warm air close to your body. A fleece or woolen sweater works well.

Outer Layer. This is your jacket and pants—the layer that keeps warm air in, lets body moisture out, and keeps rain and snow from getting in. They should be made of a windproof, waterproof, and breathable fabric such as Gore-Tex.

Other Necessities. Sturdy, waterproof gloves or mittens are an important part of the snowboarder's wardrobe. Gloves and mittens tend to take a beating, so invest in good-quality ones.

A neck gaiter, the invention that made scarves obsolete, is indispensable for keeping body heat from escaping from the neck of your jacket. The softest, snuggliest ones are made of fleece.

Goggles or high-quality sunglasses are also a must to avoid the possibility of burning your corneas and getting a serious case of snow blindness. Goggles are the best protection for stormy, windy, and low-visibility days.

And don't forget your hat.

Oops! Did I say hat? I meant helmet.

Wearing a helmet is a controversial topic among snowboarders. Some say, "No way!" Others say, "I know I should, but I don't." Wisely, a growing number are saying, "I didn't used to wear one, but now I do."

I say, Wear a helmet. They're lightweight, warm, waterproof, comfortable, and they protect your brain. Need I say more?

And while we're talking about protecting body parts, you can protect your knees with knee pads, wrists with wrist guards, elbows with elbow pads, and tailbone with butt pads. And the best thing about all this padding is that no one knows you're wearing it.

One final area to protect is your face. Wear sunblock.

Helmets are lightweight, comfortable, and protect your brain. Some, like the
Leedom, have air vents which make for cooler riding on warm days.

RENTING EQUIPMENT

Once you've decided to give
snowboarding a try, you're
faced with two equipment
choices: rent or buy.

Rent until you're sure you
like the sport enough to invest
several hundred dollars for
new equipment. So the rental
shop, whether it's at the ski
area or in a retail store down-
town, is where you'll make
your first stop.

Renting, Step 1—Forms.
First off, you'll be required to
complete a rental form. Your
signature on the front of the
form releases the shop from all
liability. Signing on the back
releases the manufacturers and
distributors of the equipment
from liability for injury, death,

A fully padded rider

Julie (left) rides goofy—her right foot in front. Regular riders have their left foot in front.

Note the different angles at which the bindings are mounted. The bindings on the freestyle board (left) are mounted at a zero-degree angle, straight across the board. The bindings on the racing board are mounted at a much higher-degree angle.

personal property loss and damage as a result of your using their equipment. In other words, if you get hurt, you're responsible, not them.

If your board gets stolen, you're also responsible. Locking it is a good idea. You can use your own lock, or most ski areas offer an inexpensive lock-up service—a dollar or two for day-long or overnight security.

Renting, Step 2—Goofy or Regular. After you fill out the rental form, you'll be asked whether you ride regular or goofy. All this means is, do you ride with your left foot in front (regular) or your right foot in front (goofy)?

How do you tell? There are several on-the-spot tests. One is to have someone push you lightly from behind. Which foot do you step onto to keep from falling? Which foot do you lead with if you slide in your stockinged feet across a waxed floor? If it's your left foot in each of these situations, then your left foot is probably your dominant or lead foot. That's the one you probably want in front when you're riding. You're regular. If it was your right foot, then you probably want that foot in front. You're goofy.

Notice I said "probably." Whatever the tests say, if you find yourself tending to ride backward, or fakie, when you first start to learn, change lead feet. There are no rigid rules—whichever *feels* right *is* right.

Here are Julie Vickery's thoughts on regular and goofy:

"I believe your dominant foot should be in front because it's the foot that controls fine-tuning and edge angles for beginning snowboarders. Historically, the dominant foot was in back because many snowboarders came from a surfing background and because of the way the boards were designed. Older boards required you to kick your back foot (stronger foot) out in order to turn the board. This is no longer the case. So the debate comes down to this: Should the dominant foot be in the front or the back?"

Renting, Step 3—Stance. Stance refers to three things: the angle of your feet on the board, the distance your feet are apart on the board, and where your feet are in relation to the tip of the board.

Stance angle is the angle at which your bindings are mounted on your board. They can be mounted straight across the board, perpendicular to the edge. That's a zero-degree angle. This is the angle that freestyle riders usually prefer.

All-mountain riders may mount their bindings at a low angle, say 15 to 20 degrees. The front binding is usually mounted at a higher degree than the back, say 15 and 5 degrees, respectively.

Racers mount their bindings at a high angle, almost parallel to the edge of the board. This faces them forward, making them look almost like a skier on one ski.

The stance that's right for you depends on the kind of riding you do. But if you're just starting out, here's what Irwin Benkert, head snowboard technician at Smugglers' Notch Resort, recommends: "Have the bindings mounted shoulder distance apart and slightly back from the center of the board. We start our beginners on a 30-degree angle on the front foot and a 15-degree angle on the back. But you can change them any time you want. The main thing is to get comfortable on your board."

One factor can influence stance: the size of your feet. People with big feet, say over size 10, can have a problem with toe drag. Their boots hang out over the edge of the board and drag on toe-side turns. One solution is to do only heel-side turns. Just kidding. Try increasing the stance angle instead.

Something else may help—a swivel plate adapter. The adapter is a half-inch-thick plastic plate that can be mounted under the front binding. It was designed to allow riders to swivel the front foot parallel to the board so they won't feel so awkward when standing in

A swivel plate adapter

line, riding the chairlift, or skating on the flats. A stationary plate is mounted under the back binding. Together, the plates raise riders half an inch, giving big-footed snowboarders more clearance for their toes.

Renting, Step 4—Trying On. The final step in the renting process is one many people don't do—try the equipment in the shop. Step into the bindings and strap yourself in. Do the buckles work? Is the ratchet action floppy or loose? Can you tighten down so that you feel securely attached to your board? Do you have room to further tighten once you've taken a few runs? Check out all these things, and if they aren't right, don't leave the shop until they are. This will save you anguish on the mountain.

Finally, are your rental boots wet inside? Wet, cold boots are a guarantee of one thing and one thing only—wet, cold feet. Ask for a dry pair.

BUYING NEW EQUIPMENT
Once you get to the stage of riding where you feel comfortable on your board, you're probably sick of renting and ready to buy equipment of your own. What's the best way to go about it?

You have several options, but no matter what you do, *try before you buy.* There are lots of manufacturers, each making a range of different boards. Your job is to find the one that's right for you and your kind of riding.

Try to demo different boards before you buy one.

So, how do you try a board without actually buying it?

One way is to take advantage of demo days at ski areas. These are days when snowboard manufacturers travel to a ski area with a van full of their equipment for people like you to try. Ask at ski shops and ski areas for demo schedules. During demo days, you can take runs on several different boards—the more, the better. There's no charge, but you have to leave a credit card as security.

•TIP• Take your own boots. Demo vans don't ordinarily carry them, and you'll get stuck renting, which takes up time. Usually, boots can't be demoed, but it's vitally important that they fit properly. So when buying boots, try on lots, and walk around in them as much as possible before you put your money down.

If you can't hook up with a demo day, another option is to talk to someone from your local snowboard shop. Many shops have programs that allow you to rent their boards and discount the money you spend on rentals from the price of the equipment you buy.

The best time to buy new equipment is at the end of the season or the beginning of the next season. That's when you'll hit the best sales.

Here are six tips from Smugglers' Notch expert Irwin Benkert for buying new equipment:

- If you're a beginner, buy a freestyle or an all-mountain board. If you plan to spend a lot of time in the halfpipe, a freestyle board may be a better choice. But both types of boards can be used for tricks, carving, and general all-mountain riding.
- A board is the correct length if, when stood on end, it reaches between your chin and nose. Let's say that's 149 centimeters. But if you can get a fantastic price on a 146-centimeter board, should you pass it up? Probably not. You can play with about 5 centimeters (that's about 2 inches) on either side and still get a board that's good for you. The two main reference points for new boarders are these: Don't choose a board that's below your shoulders; it won't have enough holding power and will tend to wash out in turns. And don't choose a board higher than your nose. The longer the board, the faster they go and the harder they are to turn.
- Buy a brand you've heard of. Some manufacturers make good-quality boards, some don't. It's safest to go with the established companies.
- Demo the board before you buy.
- If you get a great deal on last year's model, go for it. Sure, manufacturers are constantly improving their products, but there won't be that much improvement from one year to the next. As a rule of thumb, don't buy a board that's more than three years old.
- Boots are your most important piece of equipment. If you have to choose only one thing to invest in, make it boots.

BUYING USED EQUIPMENT

Okay, so you're overdrawn at the bank and your credit card is maxed out. New equipment is only a dream for you this year. Don't despair. You can get some really fine deals on used equipment at secondhand ski and snowboard sales, through the newspaper, through your best friend's buddy. Here are Irwin's seven best tips for buying used:

- Check out the edges. Look for dents. Dents, often the result of hitting hard objects like rocks or ice, could cause the edge to pull apart.

- Check the base for gouges. If there's one small gouge, don't worry about it. If there are several big, unrepaired ones, the board has had hard use. Beware. Also check for dents around the binding mounting holes. Denting is an indication that the mounting screws were too long or too short, or that the bindings were screwed down too tight. Walk on by.
- Brown, rust-colored, or whitish areas are a sign that water has seeped into the board. Be wary of water damage. This could cause the base to come apart. Avoid such boards.
- If the top of the board has large cracks, it's a sign of hard use. Walk.
- If the serial number has been scratched off, you may be looking at a stolen board. Run.

- Check the camber. Lay the board flat on the floor. If there's little or no camber, the board will have lost its zip and won't be as responsive as it should be.
- Often a used board comes with bindings. Check that the ratchets on the straps aren't loose or wiggly. Be sure the heads of the screws aren't stripped from repeated loosening and tightening. If the binding is made of plastic, make sure it isn't cracked.

KIDS' GEAR

Just a few short years ago, kids who snowboarded rode

Young riders are becoming
a familiar sight at ski areas.

a downsized adult board. Manufacturers hadn't taken into account that kids weigh less and aren't as strong. Now kids' boards are not only shorter—you can buy a 95-centimeter board suitable for a four- to five-year-old—but they're also narrower, lighter, and have a softer flex, making them easier to bend, easier to turn.

Snow sport clothing manufacturers have also caught on to the fact that dressing children correctly for snowboarding is just as important as dressing adults. Here's advice on dressing your kids from Tom Brady, director of sales and marketing for Backhill, Burton's outdoor clothing line for children:

"Dress your kids in layers. Parents often follow this advice for themselves and ignore it for their kids. Plus, they tend to overdress the kids so they get hot and sweaty. This makes layering even more important.

"I often see kids with cotton T-shirts next to their skin. This is the worst, because cotton holds the sweat. So when they come in for lunch, they're wet and hot. When they go out after lunch, they're still wet, but now they're cold. And miserable.

"Kids also need waterproof gloves or mittens, and goggles or sunglasses. I think goggles are the better choice. Even inexpensive ones are better quality than the dime-store sunglasses kids often wear."

It's not easy putting on all those darn layers all by yourself.

K elly Miller, children's snowboard coach at Stowe Mountain
Resort, offers some advice for parents:

"Parents want clothes that are durable, waterproof, and warm. They also want styles that aren't too radical, that can be worn for purposes other than snowboarding, like going to school.

"Parents often insist that their children learn to ski before they learn to snowboard. With the good equipment and instruction now available, there's no reason that a kid can't start out snowboarding. Most kids have the muscle development to learn to board by the time they're six or seven. Some five-year-olds pick it up quickly, too.

"Whatever age your child starts, give him lessons. Instructors not only teach your child what to do, but just as important, they teach what not to do. This is the way to avoid developing bad habits from the start.

"If you can afford it, a private or semiprivate lesson is best. It guarantees your child will get the attention needed to learn the skills quickly and correctly."

One final bit of advice from Kelly: "Put your kids in helmets."

3

Before Hitting the Snow

It's a beautiful blue-sky day, the thermometer hovers around 25, the mountain lies under 8 inches of new powder. You wolf down your breakfast, load your board onto the car, and hop in.

But wait, you forgot something. Something important. You forgot to warm up.

GET FIT, STAY FIT

Hitting the mountain for a long, hard day of riding without warming up makes you more susceptible to injury.

Sabrina Sadeghi in the halfpipe at the foggy, 1998 US Open at
Stratton Mountain, Vermont

Crunch

There are many ways to warm up and to get fit and stay fit for snowboarding. But I wanted to find out how a professional does it, so I asked Sabrina Sadeghi. A snowboarder since she was eleven, Sabrina won the 1994 and 1997 national halfpipe championships and was the 1995 overall FIS world cup winner. Here's her advice on fitness:

"I keep fit by staying active. The more active I am, the more energy and endurance I have. I do lots of things, not just snowboarding—hiking, skateboarding, surfing, gymnastics, biking, walking, running, lifting weights. You don't have to do all of these, but it's nice to have a variety. Then you won't get bored."

Each morning, to warm up and get her blood flowing, Sabrina goes for a brisk 10-minute walk. Her walk is followed by 100 crunches. Then, progressing from her toes to her head, Sabrina works through her stretching and strengthening routine, paying particular attention to the muscles involved in snowboarding.

Sabrina started with crunches to strengthen her stomach muscles. "It takes really strong stomach muscles to get your feet above your head, like when you're doing tricks in the halfpipe. Also, a strong stomach helps protect your back."

After crunches, Sabrina turns over to do push-ups. "I do as many as I can do. Maybe 25 or so at one time. Then I'll do another 25 later on in the day. Push-ups strengthen and stabilize your shoulders and

Push-up

upper body. They help protect you from injuries from falling and catching yourself."

With crunches and push-ups out of the way, Sabrina begins her toe-to-head workout, starting with her ankles. She holds each stretch for 15 to 30 seconds and always works opposing muscles equally—quads and hamstrings, back and stomach. Sabrina recommends doing three sets of each exercise.

Ankle Rolls. Snowboarding requires a lot of ankle movement. Ankle rolls keep ankles flexible and strong. Sabrina does 10 circles to the right and 10 to the left with each ankle, or to make it more interesting, she traces the letters of the alphabet.

Calf Stretch. You need lots of calf strength for turning and traversing. Stretching your calves will keep you from getting sore and—even worse—getting cramps.

Calf/Achilles Stretch. Together with calf muscles, you need strong Achilles tendons for turning and traversing. To give your tendons a good stretch, wedge your toes up against a wall while bringing each knee in as close to the wall as you can.

Hamstring Stretch. Strong hamstrings are especially important for lower carving positions, and they're your ACL's (anterior cruciate ligament's) best friend. You can do **lying down hamstring stretches** by pulling your calf toward your head, keeping your leg straight and

Ankle roll

Calf stretch

Achilles tendon stretch

Hamstring stretch, lying down

Hamstring stretch, sitting

pointing or flexing your toes; or **sitting hamstring stretches,** which also target your lower back and butt muscles.

Two other variations on the hamstring stretch are the **straddle stretch** and the **twist straddle.** The twist straddle focuses on stretching all the way up to your shoulders.

Straddle stretch

Twist straddle

Lunge

Squat

Lunges. To strengthen your legs, do lunges. Step straight forward and straight back, bending your stepping knee to a 90-degree angle. To avoid straining your knees, don't let your knee go over your toe.

Squats. This is another leg-strengthening exercise that also works on the back and improves balance. With your feet shoulder-width apart, your back straight, and your heels on the floor, raise and lower yourself as if you're sitting down and getting up from a chair.

Alternating back extension

Quad stretch

Alternating Back Extension. This is another good back-strengthening exercise. Lying on your stomach, extend and lift your right leg and left arm. Hold for 5 seconds. Then extend and lift your left leg and right arm.

Quadriceps Stretch. The big muscles for snowboarding are the quadriceps, which run down the front of your thigh. To stretch them, stand up straight, pull your heel to your butt, and push your hip forward.

Crossover Stretch. You'll feel this stretch in your butt, sides, and lower back. To do it, lie on your back, arms outstretched. Raise one leg and let it fall slowly to the floor, crossing your body.

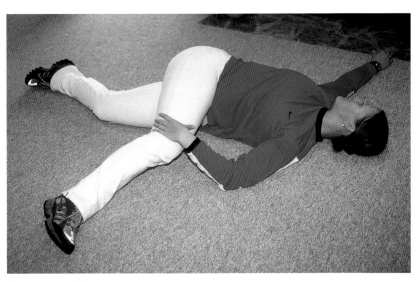

Crossover stretch

Stomach stretch

This is also a good stretch for your chest and shoulders.

Stomach Stretch. Lie flat on your stomach and, using your hands, push your upper body off the floor until your arms are fully extended. Tip your chin back.

Shoulder Stretch. This stretch limbers up the shoulders and increases their range of motion. Pull your elbow across your chest as you reach past your shoulder. Turn your head in the opposite direction.

Triceps Stretch. This is another stretch for limbering up the shoulders. Reach down your spine with one hand while you pull down on the elbow with the other.

Shoulder stretch

Triceps stretch

Sabrina plays around on the
Vew-Do Balance Board

Neck Roll. This is good for loosening up the neck. It's especially helpful if you've suffered mild whiplash in a fall. Even though it's called a neck roll, don't roll your head in circles. Drop your head forward for 20 to 30 seconds, then to the side, to the back, and to the other side.

Vew-Do Balance Board. The Vew-Do is good for developing balance skills and for practicing the foot and ankle movements used in riding, turning, jumping, and doing tricks on the snowboard. You have to keep your weight centered over your feet—or fall off. Practice balancing in the middle of the board, balancing on one side or the other, or just rocking back and forth in control.

SABRINA'S BEST TIPS FOR AVOIDING INJURY

- The best, best tip for avoiding injury is to quit when you're tired. If you hear yourself saying, "Okay, I'll take just one more run," then you probably shouldn't. Most accidents happen at the end of the day, when people are tired. It's hard to quit, especially if you're out with friends and nobody else is tired, but trust your feelings.

- Try to find the balance between pushing yourself so that you're always improving and pushing yourself too far. That's when injury happens—when you push too far.
- Build your skills slowly. At snowboard camp, kids will come up to me and say, "Hey, I want to do a rodeo flip. Show me how." I just laugh, because the kid may not even know how to turn yet. Take the time to learn the skills. You need mileage and experience on the hill. Don't try to do a rodeo flip before you've got your turns down. Learn how to ride fast before you try jumps. If you want to do spinning tricks, be able to ride fakie really solidly first.
- Make sure your equipment is right. You can't ride safely if your boots are too big, your board is too long or too stiff, too narrow or too wide. If you're a beginner, the best thing to do is to go to a reputable snowboard shop and say, "Here's the kind of riding I want to do. Set me up."
- Ask for advice, especially if you're a beginner. This is easier for adults than for kids. Kids think they know everything and are too embarrassed to ask how to do something. One way around this is to give kids lessons.
- I always advise wearing wrist and knee pads.

GET TO KNOW THE MOUNTAIN

As a newcomer to a ski area, the first thing you'll want to pick up after you've rented your equipment, bought your lift ticket, and, I hope, signed up for a lesson, is a trail map. A trail map is your pocket-size encyclopedia of the area.

Here's the kind of information you'll typically find on a trail map: a detailed drawing of the mountain's lifts and trails, plus information about equipment rentals, first aid and patrol services, lodges, snowboard events, lessons, where to shop and eat, the location of the halfpipe and snowboard park, and the skiers' and snowboarders' responsibility code.

Trail maps also show the ski area boundary. Be aware that, generally, you're liable for expenses if you snowboard *beyond* the boundary and you end up needing the services of search and rescue. If you ride on unmarked trails, say, through wooded areas *within* the ski area boundary, you're also responsible for yourself. Whenever you ride in unmarked territory, you should be an expert rider, and you should *always go with someone.*

Some areas offer ride guides. These are special guides for snowboarders that tell which runs are snowboard friendly, such as runs that don't have long, flat runouts where you could end up walking. The guides also tell the locations of the snowboard park and halfpipe, as well as runs that are particularly good for carving, bumps, trees, and steeps. Ask for a ride guide. If the area doesn't have one, someone in the snowboard school will be able to direct you to what you want.

Trail Rating. On the trail map, you'll find the color-coded system mountains use for rating the difficulty of their trails. It's especially important for beginners to know how challenging a particular trail is so they won't accidentally wind up at the top of a chute with a name like Hangman's Drop.

Be aware that the rating compares the difficulty of the trails on each individual mountain. So what may be considered an expert run on Mt. Ecstasy may be rated intermediate on Mt. Hellacious.

Here's how the color coding works:

- Green Circle: easiest trails. These trails are wide open and groomed smooth for beginners.
- Blue Square: more difficult, intermediate trails. They are steeper, usually groomed, but often narrower than beginner trails.
- Blue Square/Black Diamond: more difficult, advanced trails. Not all areas use this symbol. It means the trail is more difficult than a blue square but not quite as challenging as a black diamond.
- Black Diamond: most difficult, until you try a . . .
- Double or Triple Black Diamond: These trails are even more difficult than most difficult! These are for experts only. Extremely steep and narrow, often rock-infested, double- and triple-black-diamond trails are a no-no to anyone but real experts.

Besides being on trail maps, these color-coded symbols are usually posted on billboards at the bottom of lifts so you won't mistakenly get onto a lift that services trails you won't be able to negotiate.

ALTITUDE SICKNESS

If you're riding at an elevation that's much higher than you're used to, you could suffer from elevation or altitude sickness. Here's why.

Paying attention to these signs on the mountain will help you have a great day.

Because there's less oxygen at higher elevations, your body has to work harder to supply it to your brain. If your brain isn't getting enough oxygen, you may feel dizzy and disoriented, sick to your stomach, have blurred vision and a whopper of a headache. Any one or a combination of these symptoms usually hits within the first forty-eight hours, although altitude sickness can occur up to three days after your arrival at an area.

One of the quickest ways to help relieve the symptoms is to take oxygen. Most high-elevation areas have tanks of it at their first-aid stations.

It's smarter to avoid getting sick in the first place. Here are some hints:

- Take it easy your first day. Plan to do your sightseeing, or, if you must ride, go out for an hour or two.
- Hydrate. Drink plenty of water, even if it means having to go to the bathroom all the time. Start drinking extra water several days before your trip. This not only helps you adapt to the elevation but, if you're flying, keeps you from getting dehydrated on the flight.
- Cut out alcohol and caffeine. They're diuretics, lowering the amount of fluids in your body, the opposite of what you're trying to achieve by drinking lots of water.

MOUNTAIN ETIQUETTE

It's an exciting but rare event to be riding on a trail all by yourself. When it happens, you feel like the mountain belongs to you and you alone.

But these are fleeting moments. Usually, there are lots of other riders, including alpine skiers and telemarkers, sharing the mountain. For everyone to have a safe and enjoyable experience, it's important to use common sense and courtesy, to practice a code of mountain etiquette. This code has come to be known as the Skier and Snowboarder Responsibility Code. Here are nine of its most important guidelines:

- Ski and ride under control so that you can stop quickly.
- People below you on the mountain have the right of way. It's up to you to avoid running into them.
- Look uphill for oncoming traffic before you enter a trail, and yield to other people coming down.
- Don't take jumps unless you can see where you're landing.
- Don't stop where other people can't see you, say, under a hill. You could become a sitting target.
- Stop at the side of the trail, not in the middle, when you want to take a break. When you do stop, don't sit on your butt, facing downhill. Instead, rest on your knees, facing uphill. This way you can see oncoming traffic and get out of the way if necessary. Julie Vickery puts it this way: "Leave knee prints, not butt prints."
- Wear your safety leash when riding, walking, or skating across the flats. Wrap the leash around your wrist when you're carrying your board. A runaway board could cause serious bodily harm.
- Keep off closed trails. They're closed for a good reason, usually having to do with *your* safety.
- Because snowboarders ride at an angle to their boards, their peripheral vision is reduced when they make heel-side turns. Their heel side is their blind side. To avoid collisions, give snowboarders plenty of room for their blind-side turns.

CHOOSING AN INSTRUCTOR

In writing this book I took lessons from many different instructors. As I expected, each instructor had a different style of teaching. What I hadn't expected was that some would be better *for me* than others. I emphasize *for me* because I recognize that what *I* look for in an instructor may not be what *you* look for.

As a beginning rider, you may feel you're the last one to judge whether an instructor is good for you or not. You may not even know what to look for.

Here are some guidelines to help you make that judgment:

Ask for an AASI (American Association of Snowboard Instructors) certified instructor. That means she has been trained and certified to teach snowboarding.

A good instructor will tailor her teaching to the way you learn best. Do you like to have everything explained before you try it? Do you dispense with words and dive into action right away? It's up to you to tell your instructor what you want and need. The more specific you are, the better the lesson will be. For you.

You should feel comfortable with one skill before going on to the next. In the following two chapters, Julie will guide you through a series of basic techniques. Not all instructors will follow Julie's exact order, but you should be taught these skills early on in your lessons. And don't be afraid to say you want more practice on something or would like it demonstrated one more time.

Remember Julie's advice. Face uphill when you take a break so you can see other people on the trail.

Don't do this. It's an invitation to get hit from behind.

"The only reason I wish I was twelve years old again is so that I could try to land a 360 without fear and injury. Meantime, I'll keep trying to land it anyway."

—Martina Navratilova,
a skier since the age of three and
winner of fifty-six grand-slam titles in tennis,
who took up snowboarding when she
retired from professional tennis in 1994

A good instructor will tell you what's coming and give you an idea of how it will feel. For example, he might say that riding the T-bar for the first time may make you feel tense, like you're going to fall off. He may add that you probably *will* fall off, but not to feel bad because nearly everybody falls.

Some instructors will touch you. They'll hold your hands or put your knees or shoulders into the position they want you to take. It speeds up the learning process. But if you'd prefer not to be touched, just say so.

Some instructors will walk beside you up the surface lift, holding on to you. Then they'll walk you down again, helping you make your first wobbly turns.

Kevin Senft, snowboard supervisor at Bromley, Vermont, runs down the beginners' slope half a dozen times a day as he helps his students experience the sensation of sliding on a board. "It's no hassle," he says. "It keeps me fit."

The bottom line is that you need to trust your instructor. You need to feel willing to take chances, to try something new under her guidance. Once you feel this trust, stick with it and go back to her for refresher lessons when you need to.

From an instructor's point of view, Greg Bock, a Level III certified instructor at Winter Park Resort, Colorado, appreciates when his students tell him what they need and the way they learn best. "Some people, like me, don't care if we crash a thousand times—we just want to get out there and do it. Other people take it slower. They want things explained and demonstrated."

Greg notes that there are differences between teaching men and women. "Women tend to listen more. Men tend to be more aggressive.

Julie steadies Bill Stritzler, Managing Director of Smugglers' Notch Ski Resort, through his first lesson.

They want to get going faster. They think they know everything already.

"The exception is men who are in technical jobs like computer programming and engineering. They ask lots of questions like, 'What's my big toe on my left foot doing right now?'

"The other difference between teaching men and women is that men usually don't want you to touch them. Most women don't mind."

Greg has definite opinions about group versus private lessons. "If you can afford it, private is the way to go. You'll learn more, faster. And you can be sure the instructor is tailoring the lesson to your specific needs."

There's general agreement among instructors that people don't take enough lessons. Often they take one, then head to the top of the mountain, confident they can ride. Some can, but for most people, taking that second and third lesson can make a huge difference in confidence and style. After the third lesson, then go out and rack up the miles. When you feel you've reached a plateau, it's time to take another lesson to get you up to the next level.

Another time a lesson is a good idea is when you think you're losing ground. You've slipped back to some old techniques that you know are wrong, but you can't seem to get beyond them. A good instructor can take one look at what you're doing and straighten you out.

4

When Body Meets Board

At last you're ready to hit the snow. You feel nervous and excited as you check your boot laces one last time and pick up your board. You walk tall, knowing you look like a real snowboarder. Until you hit the learners' slope, no one can tell this is your first time out. Unless you blow the very first step, like I did.

"Uh, that's not the way to carry your board if you want to look cool," Julie admonished softly. "Like this."

In my excitement, I hadn't noticed that I was holding it with the bindings facing my side. Quickly, I flipped my board over, bindings facing out.

"That's cool," Julie said.

CARRYING YOUR BOARD

Carrying your board with the bindings facing out is one way to walk with your board. You can also hold it with both hands across your lower back. The important thing is to be sure you're attached to the leash so that your board doesn't get away from you and become a potentially dangerous projectile.

Likewise, on the snow. Unlike skis, snowboards don't have brakes built into the bindings. If you put your board on the snow and don't plan to ride right away, lay it upside down with the back of the bindings facing downhill and dug slightly in the snow. This is particularly important advice for beginners, who may absentmindedly drop their boards base-side down on the snow, and before they know it, they're halfway down the hill.

An upside down board can't run away.

•TIP• Before you buckle in for the first time, your instructor will point out the parts of the board. For simplicity and clarity, throughout this book I will refer to the part of the snowboard that goes downhill first as the tip, not the nose or the front. And I will call the edges either toe side or heel side, thereby getting rid of potentially confusing skier terminology—uphill and downhill, inside and outside edge.

STRAPPING IN

To strap in, find a level spot on the beginners' area. Level is important because on even the slightest incline, your board will want to slide and take you with it. Start by snapping the leash around your leg or onto your boot. Then strap in your lead foot. You figured out which is your lead foot when you decided whether you rode regular or goofy. Regular riders strap in the left foot first, goofy the right.

Clean out any snow and ice from the binding and from the sole of your boot. Step in, being sure to scoot your foot all the way back so

When skating on one foot, Julie pushes off with small steps so the board won't get going too fast.

that it rests against the high back of the binding. First buckle the long strap that reaches over your ankle. Make sure it's snug—this is the part of your binding that gives you the major control for turning. You may make several loosening or tightening adjustments as the day goes by.

Now buckle the toe strap. The main function of the toe strap is to keep the front of your foot from lifting off the binding so that snow doesn't build up under it. Because it doesn't affect your turning like the ankle strap, the strap over your toe doesn't need to fit as snugly.

Now that you've strapped in one foot, stand up. How do you feel? Awkward? Clumsy? Definitely. Let's face it, your foot is attached at a weird angle for moving forward. Normally, when you walk or run forward, you point your feet straight ahead, not to the side. But trust me, in a short time, even this weird, toeing-in angle will begin to feel normal. More or less.

SKATING ON ONE FOOT
Before you move forward, or skate, first take time to get the feel of the long, slippery board attached to your body. Lift it. Swing it from side to side. Whomp it on the snow. Then step with your free foot from the toe side to the heel side. Step back and forth several times. Does standing on one side feel more comfortable than the other? If so, start out skating on that side.

Skating is a skill you'll use every day that you board. You'll skate across flats to get to lifts, you'll skate through liftlines, and you'll skate away from the lift when you exit at the top of the hill. Expect to feel clumsy at first.

Get into position to skate by centering yourself over your board, with a little more weight on your front foot. The board should be flat on the snow. Push off with your free foot. Take small steps. Small is important. If you take big steps and get going too fast, you could end up off balance, with the board sliding in one direction and your free foot trying to catch up. The result? A painful split.

Push from either side of the board, whichever is more comfortable. I find there is less twisting of my front leg if I push from the toe side of my board.

Practice skating forward and in big circles, always keeping your board flat. When you feel comfortable with this exercise, get ready for the next step—a straight glide.

Before we move to the straight glide, let's talk about body stance.

CENTERED STANCE

Generally speaking, your body should be centered over the board, with your knees and ankles slightly bent, your back straight, and your hands in front of you. In this position, you have the most stability. You are relaxed, balanced, and in a position of power.

If you lean too far forward or too far back, you'll upset your balance and lose power you need to control your board. If you want to test how leaning too far forward or backward affects balance, try this: With your feet on the ground, lean forward and have a friend try to push you over. Repeat it, leaning back. See how easy it is to knock you off balance? Now stand

A centered stance like this will give you the most stability and balance.

A fully extended stance like this means you can't move further up. Not good.

A fully flexed stance like this means you can't move further down. Also not good.

with your feet shoulder-width apart, your knees slightly bent, and your back straight. In this centered stance, you're more stable. It will take much more effort for your friend to unbalance you.

Notice how Julie's knees and ankles are slightly bent in the centered-stance photo. This is the best position for riding. It allows you to move up or down to absorb variations in the terrain. If you ride with your legs fully extended or fully flexed, your knees can't act as efficient shock absorbers, moving up *and* down as you need. Think of it this way: When your legs are fully extended, you can't move up any further; you can only move down. Likewise, when they're fully flexed, you can't move down any further, only up. On a hill that's groomed perfectly smooth, you can probably get away with being locked into either of these two positions. But hit a bump, and you're in trouble. You need the flexibility of being able to move up *and* down with the changing snow conditions.

One last thing about body position: Don't lose sight of your hands. You should be able to see them at all times. If you can't, they aren't in front of you where they should be.

GLIDING STRAIGHT ON A SLIGHT INCLINE

Assume a centered stance and get ready to take your first ride.

Skate on your board up an incline. A slight incline. Stop and look around. Make sure there's plenty of space for you to come to a stop at the bottom without running into something large and solid. Point your board straight down the hill. If you don't have an instructor or some other human to hold on to, you may start gliding before you're ready. Here's a tip: Step your back foot onto the board

Resting her back foot against the binding helps Julie keep her balance when gliding straight down a slight incline.

Julie uses her toe as a temporary brake.

just in front of your back binding. Let your toe hang over the toe-side edge. Your toe is your temporary brake, keeping you from sliding before you're ready.

Once you're ready, slide your foot back off the snow. Rest it against the binding; that helps you keep your balance and gives you a feeling of stability. Get into a centered, *relaxed* stance and enjoy your first downhill ride on a snowboard! (Because she rides goofy, Julie's lead foot is her right foot. A regular rider would be riding with the left foot in the lead.)

Don't try to turn or stop. Keep gliding straight, with your board flat on the snow, until you come to a natural stop. Then do it again and again, slowly increasing the amount of incline. Each time, you'll feel more comfortable, more balanced, more relaxed on your board. Soon you'll be ready to make your first turn—the J-turn.

But first, let's discuss the concept of the fall line.

FALL LINE AND DOUBLE FALL LINE

Everybody talks about the fall line. It's an important concept, and one you should understand.

Picture this: You drive a dump truck loaded with sand into your driveway. You push the lever, and the body of the truck slowly rises. As it rises, sand slides down the back. Imagine that the body of the truck is the ski slope. The path the sand takes as it slides down is the fall line. It's the path of least resistance. A rolling ball or a stream of water would follow the same path. When you did your straight glide, you were following the fall line.

Now let's change the picture to talk about a slightly more difficult concept, the double fall line. Again, begin with a dump truck loaded with sand. But this time, jack up the left side of the truck about 3 feet. Now push the lever to empty the sand. Where does it slide? Down the back *and* to the right-hand side. That's a double fall line.

How does a double fall line affect a snowboarder? If you're riding down a hill with a double fall line, instead of gliding straight down as you did on the hill with a single fall line, you may find yourself being drawn, just like the sand, to one side or the other of the hill. Like the sand, your board is trying to follow the path of least resistance. Don't be surprised if you find yourself sliding toward the edge of the trail—and the woods! It's tricky, especially for beginning riders.

J-TURN, TOE SIDE 1. With her weight centered over the board, Julie points the board down the fall line.

J-TURN, TOE SIDE 2. To start turning, Julie puts pressure on the toe edge of the board with her front foot.

J-TURN

Toe Side. The J-turn is your introduction to turning and using your edges. Simply put, the J-turn is a straight glide with a turn at the end. The turn will be on either your toe side or your heel side. Here's how to do a toe-side J-turn.

Start on a slightly higher incline than when you were practicing the straight glide so you can build up more speed—somewhere between walking and brisk-walking speed. The idea of building up speed at this point may sound ludicrous, but trust me. Turns are easier at a faster speed.

J-TURN, TOE SIDE 3. Julie applies pressure evenly on the toes of both feet as she rides, toe-side, across the hill.

Point the tip of your board straight down the hill. Down the fall line. (Remember, Julie rides goofy, so her right foot is her lead foot.) Give a little push and place your back foot next to your back binding. Keep equal weight on both feet, bend your knees slightly, hold your back straight, and relax!

You can turn to the right or to the left. In the beginning, I found turning toe side easier than heel side. Let's assume the same is true for you. After you've gathered a little speed in your straight glide, look in the direction you want to turn. If, like me, you ride regular, you'll look to the right to make a toe-side turn. Looking in the direction of your turn is important, but don't let your torso lead the turn. Allow your feet and legs to turn the board.

•TIP• Try not to look at your feet when you're riding. The temptation is great in the beginning, but concentrate on keeping your eyes and head up to see where you're going.)

To start turning, put pressure on the toe edge of the board with your front foot. Keep pressure on the toe edge. This will lift the heel edge of your board off the snow, and you'll start to turn. That's all it takes. Once you've started turning, apply pressure evenly on the toes of both feet as you ride your toe-side edge across the hill. Stay on edge until you come to a stop.

Note: Julie emphasizes that controlling the board starts at the feet. The turning force starts at the feet and moves *up* through the legs, not from the upper body *down* to the feet. This goes for both toe- and heel-side turns.

It's important to stay on your toe-side edge throughout the turn. If you drop your heels, that's when you could catch the heel-side edge and suddenly fall on your butt.

Skate back up the hill and ride down again, repeating the toe-side J-turn until you feel ready to try heel-side.

Heel Side. The steps for turning heel-side are similar to turning toe-side. Begin gliding straight down the hill, with your back foot resting securely against the back binding. As soon as you've gathered a bit of speed, lift the toes of your front foot toward your knee. As you lift your toes, you'll put pressure on your heel-side edge and start to turn. Keeping your weight balanced over both feet, continue riding heel-side across the hill to a stop.

J-TURN, HEEL SIDE 1. Julie begins with a straight glide down the hill.

J-TURN, HEEL SIDE 2. To turn, Julie lifts the toes of her front foot. This puts pressure on her heel-side edge.

Voila! You've just accomplished three important things: You've ridden flat on your board, you've turned, and you've stopped. These three simple movements are the basic survival skills you need for snowboarding.

FEEL YOUR EDGES

When you made your J-turns, it was the first time you used the edges of the snowboard to control direction and speed. Snowboarding is a sport about edging. As you'll see, you'll be spending as little time as possible on the flat bottom of your board. So now is a good time to play around with your edges, to see how they feel.

J-TURN, HEEL SIDE 3. Julie rides, heel-side, across the hill with her weight balanced over both feet.

To feel the toe-side edge, lift your heels as high as you can off the snow.

Here's an exercise. Stand with both feet on your board, the board flat on the snow. With your lead foot strapped in, bend your knees and lift your heels as high as you can. Feel the toe-side edge dig into the snow. Now, drop your heels and lift your toes. See how high off the snow you can tilt your toe-side edge and still keep your balance. Practice going back and forth between your heels and toes, noticing the momentary stop on the flat bottom of your board in between. I call this to your attention because no matter how advanced a snowboarder you are, you can't move from

Lift your toes to feel the heel-side edge.

one edge to the other without going flat in between. You'll make this edge-flat-edge transition every time you make a turn.

WALKING UPHILL

Walking uphill with one boot strapped in can be frustrating unless you know how. Here's how to do it toe-side:

Facing up the hill, set your board on its toe-side edge across the fall line. Take a step uphill with your free foot. Pull the board up to the heel of your free foot, remembering to keep it straight across the fall line. Plant the toe-side edge into the snow so it won't slip. Take another step with your free foot. Again, pull your board up to your heel and plant the edge. Continue stepping and planting as you progress up the hill.

After you've practiced J-turns in both directions and have the feel for using your edges to turn and stop, you're ready for the next step—strapping in both feet and making linked turns—and the next chapter.

Planting the toe-side edge keeps you from slipping when walking uphill.

"I'm currently on an all-painkiller diet. 'I'll have a black coffee and 250 Advil tablets' is a typical order for me these days.

"This is because I went snowboarding.

"Snowboarding is an activity that appeals to people who do not feel that regular skiing is lethal enough.

"I took my snowboarding lesson in a small group led by a friend of mine named Brad Pearson, who also once talked me into jumping from a tall tree while attached to a thin rope.

"I now realize that the small hills you see on ski slopes are formed around the bodies of 47-year-olds who tried to learn snowboarding."

—Dave Barry,
humorist

"I second what Dave said about his inaugural attempt to learn to snowboard. Gravity certainly made its ugly presence felt at every turn (literally), and Dave's repeated bone-jarring, teeth-rattling falls on his tailbone only proved that celebrity counts for nothing when it comes to certain pursuits.

"All in all, Dave was a great sport, tolerated just enough pain to be able to write yet another hilarious Barry column (no doubt enabling him to claim a tax write-off for the entire Idaho vacation), and intelligently walked off the slope before suffering serious injury."

—Brad Pearson,
snowboard instructor

5

Getting Going

Until now, everything you've learned and practiced has been with just your front foot strapped into the binding. Things are about to change. You're going to strap in your back foot, and you're going to move higher up on the hill. But no more walking uphill. You've graduated to the lifts!

LIFTS

Ski areas operate three basic types of lifts: aerial lifts (trams and gondolas), surface lifts, and chairlifts. Some areas, like Smugglers' Notch Ski Resort in northern Vermont, have a beginners' surface lift that you can ride once you've learned the J-turn and how to stop. Julie recommends that you learn how to traverse, sideslip, and do the falling leaf before going up a more advanced lift. This chapter teaches you all those skills and much more.

Aerial Lifts. Riding trams and gondolas requires little more than carrying your board on, sitting or standing for the ride, and carrying your board off. Sometimes gondolas have an outside compartment to hold your board. Otherwise, it's up to you to hold it securely so that it doesn't knock the goggles off other riders.

Surface Lifts. The most common surface lifts—lifts where the board stays on the snow—are the handle tow and the T-bar.

The first time I rode a surface lift on a snowboard, my heart was thumping and my hands were sweaty. As a skier, I was an expert on surface lifts. But as a snowboarder, I had a serious case of beginner's jitters.

Handle Tow. This is a surface lift with handles attached to a revolving wire cable. Here's how to ride it:

- Stand next to the tow, with your front foot strapped in. Keep your back foot on the snow for balance and to stop you from

The manual lift

With her knees slightly bent and her back foot resting against the binding, Julie rides the handle tow at Smugglers' Notch Ski Resort.

slipping while you wait for the handle to reach you.

- Point your board straight uphill.
- As you grab the handle, give a little push off with your back foot so the lift won't jerk you when you start to move.
- Rest your back foot on the stomp pad or against the back binding. This will help you keep your balance.
- Hold the handle close to your hip. This also helps you keep your balance.
- Don't bend at the waist. If you need to get lower— sometimes the lift runs quite low to the snow, especially if the rider in front is much shorter than you are—bend from the knees and ankles.
- If you start to veer off the track, pressure your back foot, either toe-side or heel-side. This will bring the tip of the board back into the straight-ahead position. Once you're going straight, keep your weight evenly over both feet.
- If you fall, and most beginners do, quickly scoot out of the way of the rider coming up after you.
- Sometimes the lift will stop, usually when someone falls off. If this happens while you're halfway up the hill, step off the board. When the lift starts again, give a little push as you did when you first got on so you won't get jerked off-balance.
- When you reach the top, release the handle and skate away from the liftline, well clear of other exiting snowboarders.

T-bar. Riding a T-bar is very much like riding the handle bar lift. Here are some additional helpful tips:

- The lift attendant will slide the T-bar behind your butt. Expect a little lurch at the beginning of your takeoff and then another lurch about 10 yards later. It's that second, surprise lurch that can throw a beginning snowboarder off balance.
- *Don't sit down on the bar.* Hold the middle pole with one hand and the end of the bar with the other, and let the lift pull you up the hill.
- If you veer off the track toward a pylon, use both legs to steer or guide the board back into the straight-ahead position.
- If you feel tense, try to relax by taking several slow, deep breaths and letting your shoulders sag.
- If you catch an edge and fall, let go of the T-bar so you won't be dragged along after it. And don't worry about the bar hitting you in the head. It will recoil and continue on up the hill. Quickly get out of the track, because someone is coming behind you, probably a nine-year-old kid doing tricks on his board as he glides past, waving and grinning.
- On rare occasions, you may use a Poma lift, which is a surface lift with a round platter attached to the end of a long pole. Use it like a T-bar—don't sit down.

Chairlifts. Most snowboarders find chairlifts easier to ride than surface lifts. Even so, here are some points you should know about getting on and off.

Getting on:
- With your front foot strapped in, skate to the loading area. An attendant will be standing next to the spot where you should stop to load.

When you get onto a chairlift, hold the tip of the board up so you won't catch an edge and risk getting jerked off the lift.

- Point your board straight ahead.
- Look back over your shoulder at the approaching chair.
- Grab the vertical bar of the lift and sit down. Hold the tip of your board up so that it can't catch an edge in the snow and risk jerking you out of the chair. Lift your free foot off the snow, too.
- Lower the safety bar. If there's a foot rest, put your board on it and enjoy the ride to the top. If there's no foot rest, tuck your free foot under your board to help support it.

Getting off: Getting off the chairlift is more challenging than getting on. Here's how to make a smooth exit:

- Prepare to get off by raising the safety bar and scooting your left haunch (or right if you ride goofy) to the edge of the chair.
- Point the board straight ahead, keeping it flat in the air and the tip up.
- Place your back foot on the stomp pad or against the back binding.
- When the board hits the snow, stand up tall. Don't lean back. If anything, lean slightly forward, with a little more weight on your

GETTING OFF CHAIRLIFT 1. As Julie approaches the exit ramp, she scoots her haunch to the edge of the chair and lifts the tip of the board.

GETTING OFF CHAIRLIFT 2. She places her back foot on the stomp pad and points the board straight ahead.

front foot. Keep your hands out to help maintain balance, like a tightrope walker.

- Do a straight glide down the exit ramp until you come to a stop. Some exit ramps are steeper than others. Don't be surprised if the glide is fast and you have to do a J-turn to avoid running into someone.

The trend in chairlifts is "bigger is better." Over the years, they've grown from singles to doubles to quads to sextuplets. The eight-person lift is nearer than you think. If you're worried about getting off one of these behemoth lifts, here's what will help: First, go for the end position, either left or right. That way you'll have

GETTING OFF CHAIRLIFT 3. As soon as the board hits the snow, Julie stands up tall and glides down the ramp.

only one person next to you, not one on each side. Then, warn your fellow passengers that in the interests of their own safety, they might make every effort to avoid you when departing the lift.

STRAPPING IN BOTH FEET

Now that you've successfully exited the lift and are standing at the top of the hill, it's time to do something you've never done before—strap in your back foot. You can do it from three positions: sitting on a bench, sitting on the snow, or standing up.

More and more ski areas are providing benches at the top of lifts for snowboarders to sit on when strapping in. If there isn't a bench, you can sit down on the snow and strap in. Because snow is wet, this will result in what is known as the wet-butt syndrome.

There's a third way that leaves your butt dry. Here's how to do it: Line up your board so that it's straight across the fall line. With your front foot, which is attached to your board, slice off layers of snow until you've created a level platform. Level is important. If the platform runs slightly downhill, your board will take off in that direction when you

A fine example of the wet-butt syndrome

step your back foot into the binding—and will take you with it. Once you're sure the board won't take off, bend over and strap up. No wet butt.

Now that both feet are strapped in, stand up and look down the hill. Even though you know it's a beginners' slope, it probably looks pretty steep and scary. Take a minute to quiet your thumping heart. Several long, deep breaths will help.

Ready to start moving?

TRAVERSING

This is the movement that takes you across the hill. Let's begin with a heel-side traverse.

Julie makes a level platform in the snow with the heel edge of the board.

•**TIP**• Keep in mind that whenever I refer to standing or riding toe-side, you'll be facing up the hill. You'll be facing down the hill when riding heel-side. Also keep in mind that you can only be on one edge at a time. If you're on your heels, don't let your toes touch. If you're on your toes, don't let your heels touch.

Start by releasing your heel edge. You do this by slightly lowering the toes of your front foot. This will start the tip of the board moving across and down the hill. Look in the direction you want to go, and let the board slide. It won't be flat; because this is a heel-side traverse, the toe side of the board will be slightly off the snow. Lift the toes on your front foot to bring the board back across the fall line and to come to a stop.

Putting pressure on your front foot starts the board pointing *down* the hill. Putting pressure on your back toe or heel will bring the board more *across* the hill. Moving across will slow you down and help you stop. Some instructors use the gas pedal/brake pedal analogy to explain this front foot/back foot action.

Imagine that your front foot is the gas pedal and your back foot is the brake pedal. Push down on the gas pedal when you want to start your board moving downhill. Riding downhill means you're gaining speed. To slow down, you need to ride across the hill. Gently pushing down on your back foot (the brake pedal) while lifting off the

In a heel-side traverse, the toe-side edge is slightly off the snow.

gas will direct your board across the hill and slow you down. If you push too hard on the brake, the board will slide in the opposite direction.

Practice traversing heel-side until you can control your speed and stop. Then switch to toe-side and do the same thing. Remember to ride in a relaxed, centered position with your head up, looking in the direction you want to go.

FALLING

Yes, you will fall. And you'll do most of it during the first couple of days, which is not to say that advanced riders don't still sometimes experience the body-meets-snow phenomenon.

Reaching out straight-armed with palms open is a bad way to catch yourself in a fall.

When falling toe-side, Julie lets her knees and forearms take the impact.

Don't fall backward with straight arms and splayed fingers.

There's no perfect fall, but some falls are better than others. Here's how to make your fall hurt as little as possible:

- Keep your head from hitting the snow. This means letting a less sensitive body part take the impact. In a forward toe-side fall, let it be your knees and forearms. In a backward heel-side tumble, try to land on your butt and back.
- Don't reach out straight-armed to catch yourself. Again, let your forearms take the jolt, rather than one isolated area, such as your shoulders, wrists, or fingers.
- Make a thumb-outside fist. Landing with your palms open is an invitation to broken fingers and wrists.
- Relax and roll with the fall. A tense body is a great target for injury.

Julie advises that the way to stop taking bad falls is to take a lesson and master each skill before moving on to a new one. Also, ride on terrain that's suited to your ability. If you're falling a lot, it may be because you're on a slope that's too hard for you.

While I have you down on the snow, let's talk about getting up.

GETTING UP, HEEL SIDE 1. First Julie scoots her butt up close to the heel side of the board.

GETTING UP, HEEL SIDE 2. Then she grabs the toe side of the board.

GETTING UP

Heel Side. When first learning to ride, getting up is exhausting. The energy and muscle power it takes! But it doesn't need to wear you out if you know a few simple tricks.

Getting up from the heel side or sitting position is hard for many people. Unless you're seventeen or sitting on a relatively steep slope where gravity can come to your assistance, you'll need lots of muscle power to stand up. This three-step maneuver will help:

- Start with the board straight across the fall line so it

GETTING UP, HEEL SIDE 3. Finally, she gives a quick tug on the toe-side edge and pulls herself up.

GETTING UP, TOE SIDE I. Leading with her arm and shoulder, Julie starts to roll over.

won't slide downhill. Scoot your butt as close as you can to the heel side of your board.

- Push yourself up with one hand, while you grab the toe side of your board with the other. This helps pull your weight up and over the board.
- Give a final quick tug on the toe-side edge to pull you to a standing position.

Toe Side. This technique is often called the roll-over. It requires less energy and muscle strength than getting up from the heel side. Here's how to do it in three easy steps:

- Begin in a sitting position with your heel-side edge in the snow. With your shoulder and arm leading the way, start to roll over sideways. (There's less strain on your back if you lead with your upper body.)
- As you roll, lift your board so that it rolls with you. Keep turning until it has made a complete semicircle and is set firmly in the snow on the toe-side edge.
- You're now on your knees, an easy position from which to stand up and take off!

GETTING UP, TOE SIDE 2. She lifts the board so that it rolls with her.

GETTING UP, TOE SIDE 3. Julie continues to roll until she's on her knees.

There will be times when you'll find yourself at the top of a slope that feels beyond your capabilities. It's too narrow, too steep, too crowded, too icy, or all of the above. Don't panic. The next three skills—sideslipping, falling leaf, and garland turns—are simple to learn and will get you through conditions that would otherwise make your heart turn to ice. I call them the "you-can-always" skills after Julie's repeated reminder, "No trail is too hard because you can always. . . ." These skills are important steps in the process of learning how to turn.

SIDESLIPPING

The purpose of sideslipping is to use your edges to slide with controlled speed down the hill. In other words, sideslipping is con-

trolled braking. The only difference between sideslipping and traversing is that when side-slipping, your board travels straight down the hill (down the fall line) rather than across the hill. Here's how to do a heel-side sideslip:

- Start with your board straight across the hill, your heel-side edge dug into the snow to keep you from sliding. The toe-side edge of the board is angled off the snow.
- To start sliding, drop the toe-side edge just a little. This slight flattening of the board's angle will release your heel-side edge, and you'll begin sliding downhill.

When sideslipping, Julie's board travels straight down the hill. Notice the path that her board leaves in the snow.

To stop sliding, increase the angle of the board again by putting pressure back on your heels. Repeat this sequence—release,
slide, pressure heels, release, slide, pressure heels—until you
can do it for longer and longer distances and at different
speeds. Check out your tracks. See how little space you needed to
move down the slope? Does it feel like you're spreading smooth
peanut butter?

- Roll over and practice sideslipping on your toe-side edge.
- *Warning!* When sideslipping heel-side, be careful not to drop
  your toe-side edge so far that it touches the snow. If you do, it
  will catch and throw you for a face plant. Likewise, when
  sideslipping toe-side, watch those heels or *bam*—butt plant!

FALLING LEAF

If you imagine the zigzag path of a maple leaf falling from a tree,
you'll know how this skill got its name. When you do the falling leaf,
you'll also be following a zigzag path down the hill. Think of it as
traversing back and forth across the hill while staying on the same edge
of the board. As usual, you can do it heel-side or toe-side. Let's begin
heel-side:

- With the board across the hill, begin by stepping on the gas pedal
  (putting weight on your lead foot). This releases the edge near
  the tip of the board. If you're a regular rider, this means you'll
  start traversing to the left; goofy riders, to the right.
- To change direction, think of your back foot as your new lead
  foot (the foot now on the gas pedal). What happens? You'll traverse in the other direction, with your *back* foot in the lead. This
  backward riding is called riding fakie or switch. With the board
  turned up at both ends, it's easy to do.
- Continue zigzagging across the slope on the heel-side edge.
  Make big, long zigzags and small, tight zigzags. Then roll over
  and practice it toe-side.

GARLAND TURNS

These are a series of half turns for moving down and across the slope.
They leave a looping track across the hill that looks like holiday garland
or a rounded staircase. The sequence is downhill glide, half turn, traverse, downhill glide, half turn, traverse—until you reach the other side
of the hill. Let's begin with a heel-side garland.

FALLING LEAF 1. Julie crosses the hill to the right . . .

FALLING LEAF 2. . . . and to the left, staying on the heel-side edge.

- Release the heel edge by stepping on the gas. Turn the board down the hill by turning your front leg in that direction. The board will be almost flat, going straight down the fall line. Remember, you're making only half a turn.

Garland turns leave a looping track across the hill.

- To turn, ease up on the gas pedal (front foot) and turn your front leg so that the tip of the board heads back across the fall line.
- Continue traversing heel-side until you're ready to make another half turn.
- Repeat the downhill glide–half turn–traverse sequence all the way across the slope. Turn around by doing a roll-over, and go back, practicing toe-side garlands.

Garland turns are a good way to ease through tricky patches on the slope. And if you're feeling nervous about pointing the board down the fall line (because that's where you gain speed), practicing garlands will help you build the confidence you need.

The time has come to put together everything you've learned so far so that you can do what snowboarding is all about—linking smooth, easy turns down the hill. Get ready for pleasure.

LINKING TURNS

Let me start with a caution. One of the most common mistakes beginning riders make when first learning to link turns is to switch edges too quickly. They tend to move from one edge to the other edge without letting the board go flat in between. They forget the edge-flat-edge sequence and try to go edge-edge. The result? Catching an edge and falling.

LINKING TURNS I. Julie is on her toe side, her board across the fall line.

One reason beginning riders want to go edge-edge is the fear of gaining speed. They panic at the thought of hurtling down the mountain when the board goes flat. So practice your first linked turns on a wide, gentle slope, one where you can make big, swooping turns and not go flying between edge changes.

Now let's follow the steps for linking your first turns:

In a centered, relaxed, ankles-slightly-bent position, point the board across the hill. You are on your toe-side edge. Release the edge by stepping on the gas pedal as you did in the garland. Here's how Julie describes the next steps:

"When you can do a garland both toe-side and heel-side, you are in effect doing the beginning of one turn and the finish of the other turn as you cross the hill. The only thing missing is linking these two half turns. You link them by moving the board onto the other edge as it goes down the hill. You do this by moving your hips—your center of mass—across the board to the inside of the new turn."

In other words, Julie says, two things need to happen to link a turn: "The board needs to change edges, and it needs to pivot. To change edges, your hips, or center of mass, move across the board as your feet and legs tip the board on edge. Starting with your front foot (the gas pedal), use your legs to pivot or slide the board through the turn. To get the timing right, concentrate on moving from the edge to a

LINKING TURNS 2. She steps on the gas to release the edge and turns the board down the fall line with her front leg.

LINKING TURNS 3. Julie moves her hips across the board as she tips the board onto the heel edge.

flat board to the new edge while you pivot the board from the center with your legs.

"One way to think of the pivoting motion is to imagine you're standing on your board on top of the steering wheel of a bus—the kind of wheel that sits flat on the steering column. Using your feet and legs, you turn the wheel right, left, right, left. This is the same motion you use to pivot the board on snow. You can go onto the new edge any time you want, as long as you're pivoting the board."

Now that you know the basics of linking turns, go out and link hundreds more. As you practice, don't let setbacks set you back. Everybody has them. I had my first big one on my fourth day out. The day before, I was linking turns, no problem. Then I seemed to have forgotten everything. I felt frustrated and discouraged. Here's Julie's advice for dealing with setbacks:

- The main thing is, don't be discouraged. Think about all the things you know and do well. Don't dwell on the little things that aren't going smoothly at the moment. Give yourself lots of credit, and don't try to analyze the heck out of your mistakes. Just keep riding and have fun. That's what it's all about.
- Check your boots and bindings. Maybe they're not a good fit. It's hard to ride well in equipment that's sloppy or too tight. Is your heel lifting out of your boot or binding? Is your board too long or too short? Is it improperly waxed or not waxed at all? Any of these conditions may be contributing to your setback.
- The first time you ride a trail that's more difficult than you're used to, it can throw you off. So can riding in conditions you're not used to, like deep snow or ice. Don't panic. And don't forget the "you-can-always" skills to get you safely through tricky terrain.

It's worth repeating: Always let your board go flat before beginning a new turn. Otherwise, you risk catching an edge and making unexpected full-body contact with the snow, a.k.a. the body slam.

Don't mistake bending at the waist for bending at the knees and ankles. This is not a position of power. And it looks pretty dorky, too. Keep your back straight and your arms relaxed and out to the side.

There's a natural tendency to lean back when you get going too fast, in the vain hope that it will slow you down. But the opposite is true: When you lean back, you go even faster.

When you start a turn, if you lead with your front shoulder, look what happens to your other shoulder: It gets pulled back, and your arm with it. This is not a balanced position. Remember, you turn with your feet and legs, not with your upper body.

Take a break. Learning a new sport is hard work. Don't ride until you're exhausted—that's when accidents happen. Go out frequently, but for shorter bursts.

Don't be caught in this position!

When you feel comfortable on an easy run, try a harder one. You may struggle to get down it, but wait until you see how easy your previous runs now look. This is how you progress. Keep challenging yourself, then go back and enjoy the easier stuff. Play around with the size of your turns and the amount of sliding in your turns. Remember, this is your time off from work. It's supposed to be fun.

Don't expect your board to be angled high off the snow for your first turns. Those riders who slice down the mountain, balanced on the thin edge of the board, have accumulated lots of riding miles. For now, you should be working on low-angle skidded turns. Gradually, you'll get rid of the skid and work yourself up to the next exciting step—carved turns.

CARVED TURNS

You know a carved turn when you see one: The tip and tail of the board follow the same path, leaving a thin, clean line in the snow. And the carver is the picture of elegance—gliding, floating, skimming, deftly defying gravity.

What makes carved turns different from skidded turns? Besides enhanced elegance, carved turns mean no skidding, so slipping, no washing out—just a pure, sharp line S-ing down the mountain.

Sounds like fun? Bingo. Sound hard? Not really. You already know many of the techniques for carving; you just have to use them differently. Here are some of Julie's practice tips for minimizing the skidding of your turns to the point where there's no skid at all—the tail of the board follows the same path as the tip of the board, and you're carving.

"Try traversing across the trail, playing with the angle of your board in relation to the fall line until it cuts a clean line

**Leading with your arms and
shoulders like this is a bit fat NO-NO!**

across the slope. That's a carved traverse. Now pick a gentle, wide-open slope and, with equal weight on both feet, tip the board on edge and do a large J-turn that uses the whole hill. The size of the J will depend on the speed and edge angle.

"Remember, in a carved turn, you're on one edge during the entire turn. Therefore, edge-flat-edge still applies, but the board may be flat as you move across the hill, and it may be going onto a new edge before the fall line.

"Now go back to the carved traverse. Make a series of skidded turns linked together with a carved traverse. Try to go into the traverse sooner in the turn. Eventually, you'll be doing a carved J-turn out of the skidded turn. With lots of practice, you'll be able to carve the turn even *before* the board reaches the fall line, until the entire turn is carved.

"Practice carved turns on the easiest terrain you can find so that you can concentrate on learning the new skill, not on your speed."

As you get into carving, play around with stance angles. Sal Contreras, snowboard instructor at Suicide Six Ski Area in Woodstock, Vermont, suggested I change from 30/15 to 45/40 so that my feet would be more parallel to the edges of the board. (I was riding an all-mountain board. Riders on carving boards often set their stance angles even

The beauty of carving

"My best tip for beginners is to have a lesson and spend two or three days on the beginner slopes. People have heard snowboarding is so easy to learn, and they go to the top of the mountain on their first run. That's when they take violent falls, get hurt, and give up. They forget they're beginners, just like when they first learned to ski. And they forget they have to stay on their edges at all times."

—Heidi Voelker

higher.) In addition to the stance change, Sal offered the following carving tips for advanced riders:

"Think of your body as a piston that goes up and down, up and down. When you are in the up position, your board is heading downhill, down the fall line. When you go down, you're beginning your turn by sinking down from your knees. Your hands are out to the side, about waist-high.

"As you sink down to carve across the slope, across the fall line, try this exercise: Reach down and touch the edge of the board that's not in the snow. This will force you to drop the shoulder over the edge that's not in the snow and, by the same motion, to raise the shoulder on the carving side of the board that's in the snow. These small movements help you maintain balance by keeping your shoulders level. Repeat this exercise, both toe-side and heel-side.

"To keep your weight forward, ready to make your next turn, tuck your back knee in behind your front knee. The result is that your board will want to go into the next turn before your head will. So you've got to commit to turning earlier than you're used to. Keep practicing with your knee tucked in. Soon your head will catch up with your knees and your board, and you'll be carving long, beautiful arcs in the snow."

Graduating from skidded turns to carved turns is an exciting step. But it takes practice and patience. Begin by making big, hill-hogging turns on easy terrain, being careful not to barge into someone else's space. At first you may carve a couple turns, then skid through several more. That's okay. You're learning a new skill.

Above all, don't forget to keep having fun.

6

Beyond the Blue

One of the biggest challenges of snowboarding is the ability to change your riding to fit changing mountain conditions. Some days the mountain is blanketed in 2 feet of pristine, feather-light powder. Other days, freezing rain has frozen that powder into breakable crust and tooth-chattering ice. An ungroomed, untracked trail in the morning can be an egg carton of moguls by the afternoon.

Powder, ice, crud, moguls, trees, and the backcountry require special riding skills. Let's start with the nirvana of snow conditions—feather-light powder.

LIGHT POWDER

For your first venture into powder, pick a slope with a relatively steep incline and powder that's not too deep. You need the incline to keep up speed. (It's surprising how much resistance even powdery snow can give.) But don't play in waist-deep powder until you try knee-deep stuff. Besides the difficulty of getting into bindings, getting up from a fall in deep powder can be tricky.

To get the feel for riding in powder, imagine this: A snowboard is strapped to your feet and you're bouncing up and down, up and down on a trampoline. As you bounce up, smoothly pivot the board in the direction you want to turn. As you sink down, ride the board in that direction. Bounce up again and pivot the board in the other direction. Sink down, and ride in that direction. Try to get into the rhythm—rise, pivot, sink; rise, pivot, sink—letting your knees act as an up-down piston while your upper body just hangs in there for the sweet ride.

Keeping up your speed is essential in powder. If you've ever water-skied, think of this: The speed of the boat pulls you to the surface of the

Steve Ash floats through powder at Loon Mountain, New Hampshire.

water. When the boat slows down, you sink. It's the same when riding in powder. Slow down and you sink. So don't be afraid to point the board straight down the fall line, and for once, forget about edging. On groomed trails, getting onto the edges was the objective; in powder, you'll be riding the board flatter. Just a slight lean from one edge to the other is all you need to float through turns.

Here's another difference: On groomed slopes, you weighted your front foot slightly more than your back when initiating turns. Not so for riding powder. In powder, too much forward lean can sink the tip of the board and treat you to a powdery nosedive. Shifting your weight slightly to your rear foot will keep you out of the snow.

HEAVY, TRACKED POWDER, A.K.A. CRUD

You wanted to experience the thrill of riding virgin, untracked powder. But by the time you got to the mountain, the powder had lost its virginity to the slice and swoosh of hundreds of boards and skis. Plus, the temperature rose, and the white fluff had turned to wet, heavy powder. Don't despair. Instead, use different riding tactics.

Heavy, tracked powder—crud—can be crummy to ride in. It's bumpy and uneven. In a matter of seconds, you can go from heavy powder to hard-packed snow, then to ice and back to crud. Even with your legs acting as shock absorbers, you're bouncing all the time—crud requires a rapid, aggressive flex and extend, flex and extend. This is the kind of snow that quickly wears out your legs. Treat them to frequent hot chocolate breaks.

Steve uses his knees and ankles to flex and extend as he rides through heavy, tracked snow.

Besides taking frequent breaks, it helps to stay lower and a little back on the board. Stay low by increasing the bend in your knees and ankles. This helps you keep your balance as you speed up and slow down through the uneven snow. (Remember to bend at the knees and ankles, not at the waist.) Riding a little back elevates the tip, so when you hit deep mounds of heavy snow, the nose of the board doesn't dive and pitch you forward.

Picking a line to follow is a good idea, whether it's right down the middle, where previous riders have cleared a track, or along the sides of the trail, where it's usually the least tracked. Staying to the side gives an advantage if it's foggy and visibility is poor—use the trees as a reference point. Ride as near to the woods as you comfortably can.

And in crud, use less edge angle. Riding flatter on the base of the board lets you glide across the bumps and helps keep the tip of the board from nose-diving into a deep pile of snow. You can use those piles of snow by banking them under the board and stabilizing your turn.

Finally, relax—don't freeze up. Take lots of deep breaths, smile, and enjoy the toss and turn of a bumpy ride.

ICE

My best ice advice is simple: Avoid it. But since this isn't always possible, you want to give yourself every advantage for dealing with it.

First and foremost, tune your board for ice. That means sharp, polished edges that will grip like crazy. (It's a good idea to carry a sharpening stone with you to touch up your edges during the day. See chapter 8.) Make sure your boots are tight and your bindings are secure. The less play between your boots, bindings, and board, the more control you'll have.

Unlike riding powder, where the edge angle can be low, ice requires an acute edge angle. Flexing aggressively at your knees and ankles will increase the angle so that the edges can do what they're designed for—bite and hold on like a bulldog. It's that bite that gives you the confidence to relax, knowing that the board won't shoot out from under you. In this flexed position, your body will be low and compact, your shoulders level. Remember, you can level your shoulders by reaching for the edge of the board that's not in the snow.

Try to anticipate an ice attack by looking to see what's ahead on the trail. Sometimes you can avoid the icy patch altogether. If not, keep your weight slightly forward on the board and try to skim over

Steve sets the board at an acute angle so the edge will bite and hold on as he crosses an icy patch.

the area. The objective is to do as little as possible while you're on ice. If you must turn, make your turns big and smooth. And also be ready for a possible sudden slowdown when you come off the ice and hit a patch of snow.

If the ice and/or crud get to be too much for you, and you feel there isn't one more turn left in your body, don't forget Julie's "you-can-always" skills: sideslipping, the falling leaf, and garland turns. They'll get you through the really rough spots.

BUMPS, A.K.A. MOGULS

You can't take your eyes off him. A skilled snowboarder floating—yes, it looks like floating—down a field of moguls is mesmerizing. I had the pleasure of spending the day with such a rider. His name is Greg Bock, a Level III AASI instructor at Winter Park, Colorado. What follows is Greg's advice for getting comfortable in the bumps.

"First off, be comfortable on groomed runs before going into the bumps. You should be able to make turns of various sizes, from quick, short turns to longer-radius ones. You don't have to be carving perfect turns; round, skidded turns will get you through the bumps, too.

"Begin on terrain that's not too steep—find an intermediate run with moguls. Even better, some mountains groom one side of a trail and let the other side bump up. This is a great place to start, because you can always bail when the going gets tough or your legs start to feel like limp linguini. Look also for bumps that are nice and round, not irregular shaped and not the size of refrigerators. And keep this in mind: The turns you need to ride bumps are the same as the turns for riding the groomed. You just use them differently.

"Start by traversing across the bumps. Don't go down the hill—go across. This way you won't build up big speed, and you can practice one of the secrets of successful bump-running—keeping your board on the snow at all times. Imagine you are surfing up and over big waves, following their shape with your surfboard. It's the same on snow. Let your snowboard follow the shape of the bumps—up, over, down, up, over, down.

"Here's another secret. While traversing, try to keep your head at the same level all the time. Imagine there's a ceiling just above your head that you're not allowed to touch. But how can you avoid touching it when you're going up and down? Easy. Use your legs as giant shock absorbers, *bending* at the knees when you go *up* over a bump and *extending* when you go *down* the other side. Your legs are constantly flexing and extending, but your head never hits the ceiling. In order for this to work, you'll need to start in a slightly flexed position so you'll have a range of motion in both directions.

TRAVERSING BUMPS I. Keeping his board on the snow, Greg Bock follows the shape of the bump up,

TRAVERSING BUMPS 2. over the top,

TRAVERSING BUMPS 3. and down the other side.

As Greg Bock approaches a bump, he bends his front knee to absorb the front of the bump.

"Practice this level-headed traverse over and over, heel-side and toe-side. When you're comfortable with it, go on to the next skill—independent leg action.

"How can you use your legs independently when they're both strapped to one board? As you approach a bump, you bend your front knee to absorb the front of the bump. Notice that your back leg is more extended. Then, as you ride over the top and down the back side of the bump, look what's happening with your legs. Your front leg is now extended, and your back leg is bent. If you keep your snowboard on the snow during this exercise, your legs will naturally bend and extend, independently. This exercise will make you more aware of what you're already doing in the traverse.

"You've now practiced going across the hill, traversing the bumps. Now you want to start going down. There are three basic strategies for turning on moguls. One is to sneak around them, staying in the troughs. A second is to turn along the sides, and a third is to turn on the tops.

"Practice each strategy, turning in the troughs, along the shoulders, on the crests. Vary the turns according to how the bumps are shaped, how close they are to each other, the snow conditions, and the steepness of the slope. Also vary the size of the turns. Make quick, small turns *and* larger-radius turns as you wend your way down the slope. Remember, you don't have to go straight down the fall line. You can go wide around several bumps. You can go slow, you can go fast. It's sometimes easier to keep speed control in medium-radius turns. Round turns will be the smoothest and most controlled.

"On steep bump runs, controlling your speed is the main concern. If you want to go slower, use the shape of the turn. Fully finish your turns, even to the point of heading back up the hill. You won't be going fast for long if you're heading uphill.

"Look ahead so you can pick a path or line to follow. You may get off it temporarily. That's okay. Pick a new one so that you can work rhythm into your turns. Sing along to Jimi Hendrix and don't freak out."

•TIP• There are no rigid rules setting out the correct stance or best body position for riding in bumps, but Greg recommends the following: "Keep your weight balanced fifty-fifty on each foot, your knees slightly flexed, and your back straight. Line up your shoulders with your front foot—don't twist your upper body toward the tip of the board or the fall line. This is not a position you need to be in all the

Greg Bock turns on a bump as he glides down a field of moguls at
Winter Park, Colorado.

time; it's merely a reference point to work from. The position of your
body relative to the board will vary with stance angles."

Here are three common errors that Greg works to correct in
his lessons:

- Some riders, especially beginners, twist their shoulders toward
  the tip of the board—this points their upper body downhill,
  down the fall line. To check out how this affects the ability to flex,
  try this: Stand, strapped onto the board, with your shoulders
  lined up with your front foot. Flex. See how easy it is? Now try
  this. Turn your shoulders to the tip of the board. Flex. See how
  the ability to flex is diminished. You can't use your knees and
  legs as shock absorbers as effectively if your upper body is
  twisted to face downhill, down the fall line.
- Riding with the weight on the back foot. You've seen it—riders
  with the back leg bent and the front leg locked straight. They
  think leaning back will slow them down. This is a natural
  response, but it's wrong. Leaning back on the back foot makes
  you accelerate and propels you forward, fast. Usually this position ends in a wipeout.

- Flailing arms. You've also seen this rider, the one who uses his upper body to make the board turn. This doesn't work. Granted, there will be shoulder and upper-body rotation, but it should be used in combination with the turning motion of the feet and legs. Flinging the upper body in one direction and jerking the lower body in the opposite direction, known as counterrotation, hinders your ability to flex and throws you off-balance. It's not a pretty sight on a snowboard.

TREES AND GLADES

Snowboarders head for the trees because they know that's where there's usually a lot more snow. Plus it's quiet, sheltered, and not overrun with people. But trees are immovable objects and, as such, deserve great respect. Here are some respectful things to keep in mind when riding among trees.

For your first foray into the forest, start small—few trees, big spaces between them. Only when you're comfortable with this should you venture into tighter glades.

There's a temptation to look at the trees. Don't. *Focus on the space between them.* Cast your eyes where you want to travel, not where you're afraid the board might end up.

Don't get up huge speeds. You could snag a stump or branch or small sapling. If you catch an edge and lose control, there's little room to fall except into a tree. So keep your speed down and ride in control.

Check out your line, looking for a clear path that you can follow. Don't look at one tree at a time; rather, look at the big picture. If the extent of the big picture is no more than a couple hundred yards, ride that distance, then stop. Check out your next line.

Avoid tree wells, the area around the base of evergreen trees where, because of the branches, snow can't accumulate. Snow builds up around the trees but not in the tree wells. Dropping into one can be extremely dangerous and has even claimed some snowboarders' lives. Ride far away from wells.

Look for snow-filled streambeds. It's like finding a natural halfpipe in the woods. Follow it, gliding up one side and down the other. But be aware that you can break through the snow into the stream. Ride with caution.

Wear a helmet and goggles.

Steve Ash checks out a clear path to follow between the trees.

And most important, don't ride alone. Should you meet a tree—up close and personal—you may need a friend to help.

BACKCOUNTRY

Beyond the boundaries of a ski area lies the backcountry. You can get there by hiking, snowmobile, or helicopter. If your access is hiking, you soon learn the meaning of the phrase "earn your turns." And that's what turns many snowboarders on.

David Lines, an avid backcountry rider, describes backcountry as freedom—freedom from people, freedom from liftlines, freedom from boundaries. "One of the greatest thrills I have ever experienced is dropping into a fresh field of untracked snow. You're there all alone in the wilderness. It's completely quiet except for the occasional *whomp!* of snow falling from the branches as you glide through the trees."

But David will be the first to tell you that you need to be prepared for any emergency before you go backcountry riding, because you'll be away from people who can help you. Here are his safety tips for a day trip in the backcountry.

"Even though you intend just a day, be prepared to spend the night.

"Go with a pal. There's always the chance that you'll fall and get hurt. It could be a minor injury or something as serious as getting knocked out. In any case, a buddy is a handy thing to have around.

"Take plenty of water. Hiking up mountains takes lots of energy and produces lots of sweat. You'll lose body fluids, which need to be replaced so that you won't get attacked by your worst enemy, dehydration. To keep hydrated, don't wait to drink when you feel thirsty. Drink *before* you feel thirsty.

"Take along a change of clothes. Sweating equals wet clothes. Even if you're wearing wicking fabrics like polypropylene and capilene—and you shouldn't be wearing anything else—you'll still be wet when you reach the top of the mountain. It may seem nuts to think of stripping to the skin when the temperature is hovering around 20 degrees Fahrenheit and the wind is whipping around your ears. Okay, sometimes it's not practical to switch the bottom layer, but it still makes sense to change into as many dry layers as you can. It will make the ride down much more enjoyable.

"Take a tool kit. At the very least, it should include screwdrivers, a repair kit for your bindings, and a Swiss Army knife.

Poles can come in handy when riding in the backcountry.

"I now see ski areas from a snowboarder's point of view. How steep are the exit ramps from the chairlifts? Are there benches at the tops of the lifts where riders can sit to strap on their bindings? Are there lots of flats and traverses?

"I get treated differently by skiers. Once I took a real header, and two skiers skied close past me and said something like, 'Serves you right.' I make an effort to be overly polite.

"My secret fantasy is to do a heli-trip on a board. The last time I went, it was on skis, and because of a long-running knee problem, I was sure it was my last trip. Four others, all on boards, went on the same trip. I saw how easy it was on their knees. Now I want to go on a board, too."

—Pat O'Donnell, president/CEO, Aspen Skiing Company

"Hands sweat. Take a change of gloves. Plan to wear a light pair hiking up and a heavier pair riding down.

"Take poles. Poles? Yes, for two reasons. One, they make hiking up easier. Two, they make riding down safer. Here's how: You fall and land on your back with your feet in front of you. You try to get up by pushing with your hands. But your hands sink in up to your shoulders. There's no leverage in powder. Enter your poles. Cross them, and at the point where they meet, you have a platform against which you can push yourself up to the standing position.

"Wrap a few strips of good ol' duct tape around your pole to keep it handy for instant repairs and first aid, like finger splints.

"Pack food. Your energy gets depleted and needs to be replaced. Power bars, chocolate, s'mores, and the old standby, pb&j sandwiches, are great energy replenishers.

"Wear goggles. One tree branch in the face says it all.

"Know mountain safety and make sure there's no avalanche danger.

"Let freedom ring!"

7

Tricks and Treats

When people think of snowboarding, they imagine riders spinning off the walls of halfpipes, jumping from the top of 60-foot cliffs, or shooting over crests of enormous man-made jumps. It's the world of tricks. It's hard-core. It's freestyle. For many, especially those under twenty-five, it's the happiness zone.

But there's a growing number of riders who are over twenty-five, who aren't hard-core, and yet have an urge to do tricks. Little tricks. Greg Bock, who teaches snowboarding at Winter Park, Colorado, knows dozens of little tricks. What follows are his instructions for several soft-core maneuvers—the kind that keep your feet on the snow. The best place to practice them is on a groomed slope with a slight incline.

ON-GROUND 360-DEGREE TURN

This is a great exercise for practicing edging and balance. Start out on a toe-side turn, but keep pressuring your front foot to keep the board turning until it's actually pointing straight uphill. When you reach that point, flatten it by dropping your heels. You will now be riding straight downhill, fakie. Shift pressure to your back foot, which will start you moving down the hill. Lean back on your heels and make a fakie heel-side turn. Ride out forward. Reverse the steps and do 360s heel-side.

•TIP• Don't try to go from toe side to heel side too quickly—you risk catching your heel-side edge and stopping abruptly! Changing too quickly from heel side to toe side is also risky.

A rider in the happiness zone at Stowe Mountain Resort, Vermont

OLLIE 1. Greg Bock gets onto the tail of the board.

TWO-FOOTED JUMP

This is just what it sounds like—jumping by flexing both knees at the same time and springing up. It comes in handy when you get stuck on a flat. It may seem highly undignified to hop along like a frog until you reach the point where the board will slide again, but it's more dignified than undoing your bindings and walking.

OLLIE

This is snowboarder lingo for jumping. An ollie is a jump in which you spring off the tail of the board to get air. Here's how to do it. Beginning from a bent-knee position, jump up, lifting your front foot first and shifting your weight toward your back foot. This will

OLLIE 2. In the air, he pulls up his knees to level the board.

raise the tip of the board and get you onto the tail. From this position, you can spring off the tail to get air. As soon as it's off the ground, pull up your knees to level the board. Land flat, with equal weight on both feet. Flex as soon as you land to absorb the impact of the jump.

•TIP• You can use the flex of the board to get more height.

NOLLIE
This is an ollie in reverse. Instead of jumping and lifting your front foot, lift your back foot to get you onto the tip (nose) of the board. You can spring off the tip into the air. Again, land flat, on both feet.

•TIP• This trick is significantly more difficult. Don't be surprised if you don't get it on the first try.

NOSE ROLL
You should be comfortable riding fakie before you attempt this trick. Here's how to do a nose roll. Start out on a toe-side traverse. Shift your weight to the front foot—shift it so far front that the tail of your board comes off the ground. Look downhill and swing the tail around 180 degrees in an uphill direction. Make a fakie toe-side turn out of it.

If you learn to ride in fakie and out forward, you can make linked forward and fakie toe-side turns.

•TIP• Be sure to flex your knees as the board touches down.

180-DEGREE TURN
This trick is slightly more advanced than the nose roll because there is more potential for catching an edge and crashing. Again, you should be comfortable riding fakie before you try 180s. Start on a toe-side traverse. Flex down, spring up, look down the hill, and rotate 180 degrees so that the tail of the board spins uphill. Flex your knees to absorb the landing and make a fakie toe-side turn out.

HALFPIPE HISTORY
Not long ago, the halfpipe—a long snow trench—was an unknown commodity at a ski area. But after snowboarding took off in the early

Jim McDowell uses the halfpipe grinder to shape the walls of the pipe at Smugglers' Notch Ski Resort in Vermont.

nineties, ski areas hurried to accommodate this new clientele. One of the ways they did it was by building halfpipes.

With many snowboarders coming from a skateboarding background, something like a skateboard halfpipe was bound to appear. Early halfpipes were inexact affairs. Shovels and rakes were the main tools, and muscles the main power. Then came the invention of the halfpipe grinder, and things changed dramatically.

Attached to a snowcat, the grinder shapes the walls of the pipe, shaving off small amounts of snow at a time. I watched the process from the passenger seat of a snowcat while Jim McDowell, terrain parks coordinator at Smugglers' Notch Ski Resort in Vermont, made several passes through the pipe. He explained that designing a halfpipe is a real skill, something that's taken him years of practice.

"The measurements have to be standard. The best pitch or slope is about 15 degrees. The pipe should measure between 45 and 60 feet from rim to rim and between 25 and 35 feet across the flat bottom. The walls stand at approximately 10 to 12 feet high. Most areas aim to have their pipes 300 to 350 feet long."

Jim says that riders don't hesitate to give him feedback all the time. "They don't want the lip too steep or too shallow. They don't like it when the walls are rutted."

Jim grooms the pipe about once a week, depending on the amount of use and the weather. He uses the grinder at the end of the day so that the colder nighttime temperatures will freeze the snow and help maintain the shape.

DEMYSTIFYING THE HALFPIPE

There are many riders, especially those over twenty-five, whose closest encounter with a halfpipe is walking along the deck, watching other riders. They feel they don't have the skills or the guts to drop in and give it a go. But as Jim Broda, manager of the Snowboard School at Stratton Mountain, Vermont, explains, "Riding the pipe doesn't necessarily mean taking big air. It can be just playing around on the bottom and low side walls. Some areas, like Stratton, have built mini or quarter pipes, which are smaller versions of the halfpipe. Some call them 'half-pints.' They're great for getting the feel for riding the pipe.

"You use the same maneuvers in the quarter pipe that riders use in the halfpipe, but your board never has to leave the snow. I call it 'half-pipe for over twenty-fives.' Here's how to do it.

"Approach the wall of the quarter pipe on your toe edge. At the high point of the wall, turn as you normally would, except put more

HALFPIPE MANEUVER 1. Jim Broda demonstrates how to approach the wall of the pipe on your edge.

HALFPIPE MANEUVER 2. At the high point, pressure your back foot to help pivot the board.

HALFPIPE MANEUVER 3. Ride down the wall on your heel side.

pressure on your back foot to pivot the board. This turns you onto your heel side to ride down the wall." Jim compresses his body by bending his knees as he rides on his toe side, then extends his legs at the transition or turn, then compresses again as he rides down on his heel side.

"When riders take air in the pipe, they're doing the exact same maneuver. They approach the wall on the toe side, launch off the lip of the pipe, pivot or twist in the air, land flat on the board, then ride heel-side straight down the wall. Remember, only after the flat landing do you get onto your heel edge. Also, be sure to look over your shoulder at the opposite wall—where you're headed—at the apex of your turn.

"Believe it or not, this is just a variation on the turns you make all the time. You're just doing it against a wall or in the air. It's such fun, you might surprise yourself and graduate to the halfpipe. If you do, be sure you know how to comfortably link turns, ride fakie, and do 180-degree turns."

It's beyond the scope of this book to teach advanced maneuvers like spins, grabs, handplants, aerials, and the many variations of each that can be performed in the half-pipe. The best way to learn these techniques is to go to a snowboard camp. And camps aren't just for winter riding. Mount Hood in Oregon gets so much snow that you can attend camp there during the summer months. Check out the list of camps in chapter 9.

SNOWBOARD PARKS

Most ski areas incorporate the halfpipe into a snowboard park. Besides the halfpipe, parks can include things like

Catching air in the snowboard park at Tremblant, Quebec

ramps, rails, boxes, tabletops, and old cars embedded in the snow. And there are always humongous jumps to satisfy that urge to take air. If you have that urge, here are some things to keep in mind for a safe landing:

- Case out the bumps before you ride them. See how close one lies behind the other—and what the landing between them is like.
- Be sure there are no other riders farther down on the jumps that you might collide with.
- Know where you're going to end up before you take off. Landing on the flat can seriously hurt your knees, ankles, and back. Be sure to land with bent knees on an incline.

BORDER-CROSS

Picture this: Anywhere from four to eight riders, all taking off at the same time, charge through a course of bumps, turns, and obstacles with the sole objective of beating their opponents to the bottom. It's border-cross—a free-for-all on snowboards. Competitors have to stay inside the boundaries of the course, but shoving and pushing are part of the fun. And don't think border-cross is just for freestylers. Anyone with a board strapped to his feet, who enjoys a sudden rush of adrenaline, should go for it.

To avoid injury, be sure to land a jump with bent knees on an incline.

Border-cross—a fun free-for-all where manners take a back seat

Hugging a gate at the 1998 US Open in Stratton, Vermont

"My image of snowboarding is changing. Why? There's more crossover of skiers into the sport, more parents and children are getting into it. I think there's growing respect between riders and skiers. Plus, the grunge look isn't quite as strong as it used to be."

—Heidi Voelker

RACING

Unlike border-cross, racing is a highly structured event where riders make precision turns around preset gates, often at very high speeds. The racer with the fastest speed wins. Some of the races include the slalom, giant slalom, and super-giant slalom. Here's how to tell the three slaloms apart: Slalom gates are set closest together; giant slalom gates are set farther apart, and super-giant slalom are set farthest apart of all.

Because the gates are far apart in the super-giant slalom, racers make fewer turns and therefore reach the highest speeds—sometimes up to 70 miles an hour. Giant slalom racers make turns but still can reach speeds of 40 to 50 miles an hour. Slalom racers make many, very quick turns through a series of closely placed gates that run down the fall line. The goal for all three types of races is to be the first across the finish line.

Don't let the phrase "often at very high speeds" discourage you from racing. If you're competing for fun in an amateur race, you'll have a blast. And there's no better way on snow to improve your riding skills and build your confidence.

8

Chris and Jim's Excellent Tuning

One of the biggest favors you can do your riding is to keep your board well tuned. Hard-core snowboarders do it. Most casual riders don't. They get their boards tuned at the beginning of the season—maybe— and forget about it until the next season. Bad idea. A tuned board is easier to turn, glides better (especially over the dreaded flats), and even more important, lasts longer.

Tuning a snowboard yourself isn't hard. In fact, it can be fun and extremely satisfying. All it takes is a few inexpensive tools, light elbow grease, your favorite CD, and about half an hour.

I spent an afternoon with two guys at Burton Snowboards—technician Jim Wood and Chris Mask, director of sales and marketing for RED. Jim and Chris went through the steps of do-it-yourself tuning. What follows is their expert advice.

Tools of the trade (left to right): snowboard vise, waxes, file guide, file, P-Tex candles, fibertex pads, scraper, steamless iron

WORKSPACE

A workshop is ideal. If this isn't available, find a room that's well ventilated, has good lighting, and that you don't have to worry about messing up with cleaning solvents, hot wax drippings, or metal filings.

TOOLS

The basic tool kit includes a file; file guide; file card or brush; soft (rubber), diamond, and ceramic deburring stones; scraper; wax; P-Tex candles; brass brush; nylon or fibertex pads; a steamless iron; and, if you can afford it, a snowboard vise. I'll explain the use of each of these items throughout this chapter.

EDGE FILING

There are two metal edges on a snowboard, the base edge and the side edge. Before filing them, you should first get rid of any burrs. Burrs are those little blood-letting nicks in the metal caused by hitting hard objects like rocks.

Lay the board deck-side down, and run the rubber deburring stone along the base and side edges. Work from tip to tail in a back-and-forth motion, until the edges feel pretty smooth to the touch. Then you're ready to start filing.

Begin filing the base edge first. Place the file flat on the base at about a 30-degree angle. Starting at the tip, pull the file toward you in smooth, long, even strokes as you work down the entire length of the board. Don't move the file back and forth. Work in one direction. Clean the file with a file card or file brush before moving to the other base edge.

After you've filed both base edges, smooth off any roughness, first with the diamond stone, then with the ceramic stone. (Diamond and ceramic stones work better if you use them wet. Store them in a cup of cold water.) The ceramic stone has two sides; begin with the dark, coarse side and finish off with the white, finer side. Unlike filing, you can run the stones back and forth in both directions.

Now turn the board to file the side edges. (Here's where the snowboard vise is particularly handy.) To hold the file steady and to be sure you're filing at a 90-degree angle (or at the angle you set), slip the file into a file guide. Again, file in one direction only. After filing each side edge, finish by smoothing off with the diamond and ceramic stones.

Now that the edges are nice and sharp, the next step is to dull them. What?

Filing the base edge

Actually, you want to dull, or detune, just a small section of the edges at the tip and tail. Detuning helps keep the board from turning before you're ready, thereby avoiding that unpleasant catch-an-edge maneuver.

Using the soft, rubber deburring stone, smooth the curved-up edges (the shovel) on both sides of the board. Work from the tip back to the contact point—the point where the board first touches the snow. Dull the tail edges in the same way. Beginning riders may want to detune back a couple additional inches. This will help them not catch an edge. The amount you detune is up to you and your style of riding. Play around with it until it feels right.

Smoothing the edge with a diamond stone

1. Smoothing the edge with a course ceramic stone,

2. followed by a fine ceramic stone

3. Filing the side edge using a file guide

4. Detuning with a soft stone

BASE REPAIR

If every day was a powder day, there would be little need for base repairs. But gouges happen, and minor, surface ones are easy to repair with P-Tex, a polyethylene-paraffin mix in the shape of a pencil.

Begin by cleaning out the gouge. With a metal scraper, clean off any rough bits around the damaged area. Shape the gouge into a V-shape so that the P-Tex can run evenly down the slanted sides.

If the P-Tex candle has been used before, cut off any old black carbon residue. The repair must be clean, not contaminated with carbon. Light the candle with a match or pocket lighter. Holding the lighted P-Tex close to a metal scraper will make it burn blue (hotter) and keep carbon from building up. If carbon does appear, rub it off by twisting the lighted candle against the edge of a metal scraper.

To make the repair, hold the P-Tex candle close to the base, which keeps the flame burning blue and clean. It also lets the P-Tex roll, not drip, into the gouge. If the hole is quite deep, you may need to make several passes back and forth, building up thin layers of P-Tex as you go. You don't need to let it cool between passes. Keep adding P-Tex

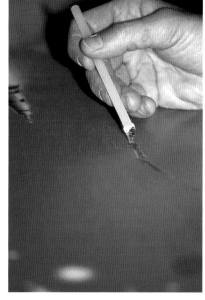

Using a metal scraper to clean carbon off a P-Tex candle

Repairing a gouge with P-Tex

Scraping P-Tex with a metal scraper

until it's slightly raised above the base of the board. Let it cool to room temperature. Then, using a metal scraper, scrape off the P-Tex until it's even with the base. A sharp scraper works best. Keep it sharp by filing it, then deburring with the soft, rubber stone.

A dirty repair doesn't adhere well. Should you accidentally drip carbon in the gouge, extinguish the P-Tex candle, clean out the dirty repair, and start over.

Make sure the room is well ventilated so you don't breathe in P-Tex fumes. It's safest to wear a mask. And be careful not to drip hot polyethylene on your skin. It burns.

WAXING

There's no such thing as waxing too often. The ideal is to wax every day that you ride. Most people don't come near that ideal, but they should aim to wax at least after every two or three days of riding.

To get the most out of your wax job, choose a wax that suits the snow conditions, whether it be bone-crunching ice or soupy spring mush. For new or harder snow, use a harder, cold-temperature wax. For softer, wetter snow, use a wax for warmer conditions. Hard-packed snow and ice wear wax off faster than soft snow, so be prepared to wax more often when riding the hard stuff.

The first step in waxing is to clean the base to get rid of dirt, muck, and old wax. You can do it two ways. One is by using a spray-on, wipe-off solvent. (Solvents and waxes can give off nasty fumes, so be sure to have the workspace well ventilated.) This is the easier way and probably the more common, but Chris advises against it. "Solvents aren't good because they dry out and oxidize the base—just the opposite of what you want. Using wax as a cleaner is a much better way to go."

1. Applying wax with a hot,
steamless iron

2. Spreading melted wax evenly on the
base of the board

3. Scraping excess wax

Structuring the base with a brass-bristled brush

Here's how to apply wax to a board, whether it's for cleaning or for riding. If it's for cleaning, use a hydrocarbon wax. If it's for riding, select a wax to suit the snow conditions.

First, make sure the board is at room temperature before you work on it. Turn the iron to a medium setting. It needs to be warm enough to melt the wax, but not so hot that the wax smokes. Hold the wax against the tip of the iron, letting it drip in lines (or creative patterns!) as you move slowly up and down the board. Apply enough wax to end up with a thin, even layer all over the board once you've smoothed it out with the hot iron. Keep the iron moving so that no one spot becomes overheated.

If you're waxing to clean the board, scrape the wax *before* it cools. If you're waxing to ride, scrape it *after* it cools. In either case, work from the tip to the tail, pushing the scraper away from you. You don't need to scrape too hard. You're done when no more wax builds up in front of the scraper. Finish by polishing with a nylon or fibertex pad.

Now you're ready to ride . . . unless you want to do one more technical, but easy, step. You can structure the wax. Structuring the wax is putting lines or grooves in it to help break up the friction and suction caused when the board moves over snow. Structuring lets the board glide more easily, so it's a good idea to do it.

Using a brass brush, go back and forth at about 45-degree angles across the base, drawing brush lines in the wax. Work in overlapping strokes to create a sort of crosshatch pattern from the contact point at the tip to the contact point at the tail of the board. When you're finished, wipe off the bits of roughed-up wax with a clean cloth, and polish with a nylon or fibertex pad. Now you're really ready to ride!

PORTABLE TUNE-UP

If you're in a hurry or away from your workshop and you don't want to fork over the money for a shop tune-up, here are a couple of simple things you can do at the end of each day of riding to keep your board in shape. One is to run a diamond stone over the edges to smooth out nicks and burrs. This takes just a minute, and the stone is light enough to carry in your pocket.

The second is to apply a fluorinated paste or rub-on wax that you can pick up at a ski or snowboard shop. It doesn't have the staying power of hot wax, but it's better than riding waxless. And you can stick it in your pocket, along with the stone.

SUMMER STORAGE

At the end of the season, put your board to bed under a thick blanket of wax. Hot waxing will seal in moisture and keep the base from drying out in the summer heat. Be sure to cover the metal edges with wax to prevent rusting from humidity. Store the board in a plastic bag or in a snowboard travel bag. Or you can chuck it under your bed with all the other stuff that's under there.

You can take the bindings off the board or leave them on. Either way, buckle them up.

If you have soft boots with inner bladders, take the bladders out and thoroughly dry them at room temperature, not close to a heater. Once dry, put the bladders back in and tie the boots. They'll hold their shape better if they're tied. Store your hard boots buckled for the same reason.

DON'T-DO-IT-YOURSELF REPAIRS

Some repairs require the tools and expertise of snowboard technicians like Chris and Jim. Three such repairs are deep gouges, delamination, and an unlevel base.

"I started snowboarding at Snow Summit when I was sixty-two. Some of Burton's riders were there doing demos, so I took a lesson. They could ride, but they couldn't teach. I kept on riding by myself and got pretty banged up—headaches, bruised shoulders, sore wrists. But it became a challenge I had to master.

"After about twelve hours of hard work, I started to have fun. Eventually I got certified as a snowboard instructor in PSIA Rocky Mountain. It was the first exam ever given for snowboard instructors.

"The sport is changing. It has lost its counterculture cachet because of old folks like me getting into it. Who do I consider old? Anybody over thirty-five. Sure, commercially it's good, but the essence of boarding is being destroyed. It's become the thing to do rather than the thing *you* do."

—Doug Pfeiffer,
inducted into the Ski Hall of Fame
for his contribution to the sport of skiing,
editor of *Skiing Magazine* from 1963 to 1976,
and author of four books on skiing technique

Deep gouges are gouges that extend through the base into the core of the board. A P-Tex repair won't hold up. Make an appointment with your own Chris or Jim.

A snowboard is made up of four layers—the base, the core, the metal edges, and the top deck. They're all glued together. If any two of these layers come unglued, they're delaminating. Get thee to a shop.

Surprisingly, a new board straight out of the shop may have a base that's not level with the edges. Sometimes the edges are higher than the base, sometimes lower. You, or your snowboard shop, can check for levelness by rolling a true bar—a round metal dowel—down the length of the board. (A level or straightedge will do if you don't have a true bar.) If you see light between the board and the bar, the base isn't level with the edges. When you're riding the board, it may hook or veer off unexpectedly, or it simply may not track straight. An unlevel base is easy to diagnose but needs the expertise of a snowboard technician.

Jim uses a true bar to check the board for levelness.

9

Staying in Touch

This chapter includes organizations, camps, videos, publications, and websites that you can consult to learn more about snowboarding, as well as websites that publish avalanche information.

ORGANIZATIONS

For information on people and products:
SnowSports Industries American (SIA)
8377-B Greensboro Drive
McLean, VA 22102-3587
703-556-9020
fax 703-821-8276
fax-on-demand 800-730-3636
www.snowlink.com

American Association of Snowboard Instructors (AASI)
133 South Van Gordon Street, Suite 101
Lakewood, CO 80228
303-987-9390
www.aasi.org

United States Ski & Snowboard Association (USSA)
P.O. Box 100
Park City, UT 84060
435-649-9090

CAMPS

Delaney Snowboard Camp
Beaver Creek and Crested Butte, CO
800-743-3790
www.delaneysnowboard.com

Windell's Snowboard Camp
Mt. Hood, OR
800-765-7669
www.windells.com

Camp of Champions
Blackcomb Mountain, BC, Canada
888-997-camp
www.campofchampions.com

Mt. Hood Snowboard Camp
Mt. Hood, OR
800-247-5552
www.snowboardcamp.com

High Cascade Snowboard Camp
Mt. Hood, OR
800-334-4272
www.highcascade.com

United States Snowboard Training Center
Mt. Hood, OR
800-325-4430
www.snowboardtraining.com

VIDEOS

The Secrets of Freeriding
Snowboard Life
800-788-7072

Dial Tune
A snowboard tuning and maintenance guide.
800-721-TUNE

Boarding Essentials
An instructional video for beginning and intermediate riders.
Freestyle Productions
675 NW Country View Rd.
White Salmon, WA 98672
800-805-8580

TB 6 Carpe diem
A video of extremely daring riding and extremely good photography.
Standard Films, produced by Mike Hatchett
530-546-4804

No Man's Land
Features female-only skiers and snowboarders.
Radical Films Inc.
103-4338 Main Street, Suite 128
Whistler, BC VON 1B4 Canada
877-RAD-FILM

Transworld Snowboarding Magazine is available on video three times a year. The video features footage based on the magazine. *Snowboard Life* also produces videos. The latest is called *Snowblind*. Both magazines have forms for ordering videos, or call Transworld Snowboarding, 800-788-7072, ext. 110.

PUBLICATIONS

Warp Magazine
P.O. Box 469014
Escondido, CA 92046-9019
888-897-6247
www.twsnow.com

Eastern Edge
P.O. Box 480
Stowe, VT 05672

Transworld Snowboarding
P.O. Box 469019
Escondido, CA 92046-9019
888-897-6247
www.twsnow.com

Fresh and Tasty Magazine
100 Spring Street
Cambridge, MA 02141
617-547-6520

Snowboarder
33046 Calle Aviador
San Juan Capistrano, CA 92675
949-496-5922
www.snowboardermag.com

Snowboard Life
353 Airport Road
Oceanside, CA 92054
760-722-7777
www.twsnow.com

Sno Magazine (English language, Canadian publication)
850, Bernard-Pilon
McMasterville, Quebec, J3G 5X7, Canada
514-464-3121

SQ (French language, Canadian publication)
850, Bernard-Pilon
McMasterville, Quebec, J3G 5X7, Canada
514-464-3121

Snowboard Canada
2055 B Queen Street East, Suite 3266
Toronto, Ontario, M4E 1G3, Canada
416-406-2400

WEBSITES

www.twsnow.com
For information on magazines, music, Olympics, manufacturers, forums/chats, events, pro bios, resorts, snow reports, and products.

www.snowlink.com
This is the SIA website. It gives information on equipment, clothing, lessons and demos, competitions, clubs, and products. It serves the sports of snowboarding, snowshoeing, and downhill and cross-country skiing.

AVALANCHE INFORMATION

Forest Service National Avalanche Center
www.avalanche.org/~nac/

Cyberspace Snow and Avalanche Center
www.csac.org/

Avalanche!
usforest.com/forest/regions/2/whiteriver/edu/avalanche/index.html

Snowboard Trivia

1. In snowboarders' lingo, "It's sick!" refers to
   a. something really exceptional
   b. something really disgusting
   c. a beginners' trail

2. In the decade between 1987 and 1997, the number of snowboarders in the United States
   a. nearly doubled
   b. nearly sextupled
   c. nearly quadrupled

3. Who invented the high-back binding?
   a. Jeff Grell
   b. Jake Burton
   c. Tom Sims

4. Who started by designing a 45-pound snowboard and later developed the original Winterstick?
   a. Sherman Winterston
   b. Dimitrie Milovich
   c. Tom Sims

5. The first National Snow Surfing Championship held at a ski area took place in 1982 at
   a. Snowmass Ski Area in Colorado
   b. Sugarloaf Ski Area in Maine
   c. Suicide Six Ski Area in Vermont

6. Two brother who were early pioneers in designing
   snowboards with metal edges were
   a. Steve and Dave Derrah
   b. Tom and Bill Sims
   c. Jake and Phil Carpenter

7. What well-known rider was a movie stunt double for Agent 007?
   a. Ross Rebagliati
   b. Tom Sims
   c. Jake Burton Carpenter

8. Who won the first Olympic gold medal in snowboarding?
   a. Ross Powers
   b. Ross Chiollatti
   c. Ross Rebagliati

9. What caused the disqualification of the first Olympic gold-medal
   snowboarder at the 1998 Olympics in Nagano, Japan?
   a. taking anabolic steroids
   b. inhaling secondhand smoke
   c. listening to Jimi Hendrix and Jim Morrison

10. A rotational air in the halfpipe is where the rider
    a. rotates the board 360 degrees or more
    b. rotates the board 720 degrees or more
    c. rotates the board less than 180 degrees

11. In 1996, male snowboarders outnumbered
    female snowboarders by about how much?
    a. three to one
    b. ten to one
    c. fifty to one

12. In snowboard lingo, boning is
    a. missing a trick and landing on your tailbone
    b. elbowing another rider off his board
    c. straightening out one or both legs when doing a trick

13. Ask to see a Chicken Salad and you'll see
    a. a boarder flapping his arms as he executes tricks in the halfpipe
    b. a boarder grabbing his board through his legs
    c. a boarder landing on his hand on the lip
       of the pipe and making chicken noises

14. In snowboard lingo, a Slob refers to
    a. snowboarders' baggy fashions
    b. a trick on the frontside wall of the halfpipe
    c. a really sloppy run in the pipe

15. Which three-time halfpipe world champion
    boycotted the 1998 Olympics?
    a. Jim Morrison
    b. Terje Haakonsen
    c. Jeff Brushie

16. Which halfpipe trick features a 540-degree rotation?
    a. a McTwist
    b. a Roast Beef
    c. a Stale Fish

ANSWERS TO SNOWBOARD TRIVIA
    1. a
    2. c
    3. a
    4. b
    5. c
    6. a
    7. b
    8. c
    9. b
    10. a & b
    11. a
    12. c
    13. b
    14. b
    15. b
    16. a

Index

Page numbers in italics refer to illustrations and sidebars.